NY Times Best-seller
MARC SHAPIRO

KEANU REEVES'
EXCELLENT ADVENTURE
An Unauthorized Biography

For more information contact:
Riverdale Avenue Books
5676 Riverdale Avenue
Riverdale, NY 10471

www.riverdaleavebooks.com

Design by www.formatting4U.com
Cover by Scott Carpenter

Digital ISBN: 9781626015609

Print ISBN: 9781626015692

First Edition August 2020

TABLE OF CONTENTS

AUTHOR'S NOTES
JUST A REGULAR GUY

The first time that I met Keanu Reeves was in 2003 during a Los Angeles press conference for the third installment of *The Matrix* film series, *The Matrix: Revolutions*. My initial impression was that glad-handing the press and making happy-talk about his latest film while paparazzi were clicking and shuttering images of the event was the last thing Reeves wanted to do.

Although he was the star of the film, his body language and painfully shy smile pointed to an actor doing his best to fade into the background. Shifting uneasily in a chair and trying to hide behind a microphone, you had to feel for the guy. You knew that chit-chatting with the assembled press while attempting to look relaxed—as he was blinded by paparazzi flash and camera click—was definitely not his thing. And to be fair, the media in attendance knew it as well.

Reeves' responses to questions were concise, if not overly insightful or earthshaking. He was polite and seemingly eager to please, but displayed none of the ego and arrogance we've come to associate with stars of his caliber. His matter-of-fact tone was less easy than calculating and predictable; far from the usual softball responses offered up by Hollywood. Keanu Reeves was more than willing to get out the word on the film. It was his job, and he's always been someone who would step in and do something to help the cause.

But as the press conference concluded, Reeves, politely, after a few handshakes and some informal "happy talk" with his fellow actors, was out the door and into the day. Where he was going was anybody's guess.

Perhaps he went to walk on the beach, ride his motorcycle on winding roads in the Hollywood Hills, visit a nearby art gallery or walk the city streets alone, deep in thought. Because while Keanu Reeves knew his place in the world of celebrity, he also worked hard to maintain the truth that in his heart and soul, he was just a regular guy.

There seemingly has never been a rhyme or reason to Keanu Reeves. In the best of times, Keanu could appear lost in his own thoughts, or a bit oblivious He's mystical in attitude, spiritual in an earthy sort of hippie, punk-rock way. Yet he's definitely made some wise choices when it's come to career, even if those choices were often more luck and happenstance than calculating Hollywood hustle.

If he never did anything beyond *Bill and Ted's Excellent Adventure*, *Speed*, *The Matrix* and, recently, the *John Wick* action movies, he'd be in the hall of fame 10 times over. He's had his share of clinkers and borderline stinkers, as well as some good work in obscure foreign and art films, many of which came and went with little recognition or public impact. If he liked the role, Reeves took it. Simple as that. And the consequences of his choices be damned.

It would take a film completist of the nth degree to pronounce any one film as his signature performance. If you blinked, you missed two of his more under-appreciated efforts as the stoic, subtly worldly everyman in *Johnny Mnemonic* and *47 Ronin*. And if you'd bet the farm that Reeves could not do wry, expansive humor, you'd lose because of the direct-to-cable romantic comedy *Always Be My Maybe,* in which Reeves did a hilarious turn playing himself.

Keanu Reeves has wandered through his life and times in such a lowkey manner that observers have often wondered aloud just how he can be so normal. But the fact remains that by Hollywood standards he is just that.

Reeves does not travel with a posse. If you catch him on the likes of *TMZ* or the other tabloid celebrity shows, odds are good that he was simply walking through the frame.

He is wildly approachable and friendly to the max. It is not unusual for Keanu to engage strangers and fans as if they were long-lost friends. He is generous with his time, uses his money wisely in the support of numerous charities, and remains humble in the face of the accolades that, in recent years have painted him as both one of the sexiest men alive and one of the nicest guys on the planet. If you're looking for a Boy Scout, Reeves fits the bill, more or less. Because lurking below the surface has always been the wild child, giggling as it attempts to get out.

But it has not been, pardon the cliché, a bed of roses. Reeves has experienced disappointments, tragedies, dysfunction and loss; in other words, all the ups and downs of human life and experience. Any author attempting to write a book on Keanu Reeves ends up facing a monumental challenge.

Contemplating *Keanu Reeves' Excellent Adventure: An Unauthorized Biography* forced me to be of two minds. He has a cool personality; he's definitely not a by-the-numbers kind of guy. He has an interesting philosophy, a Tao of Keanu, if you will. He is a much under-appreciated actor who consistently does good to great work. But there was also that little matter of his being a genuine human being. There would be no room for B.S. in this book. It would be an emotional and psychological journey through a minefield. And some of the mines would explode.

I couldn't say yes fast enough.

One could easily do the complete life and redundancy of a Keanu Reeves. I love movie-making anecdotes just like the rest of you, but I'll be the first to admit that books which go that route often tumble into a blur of repetition and sameness. You know the drill: The director was a wonderful human being. The script was a work of art. The entire cast and crew were princes and princesses for the ages. Get the picture?

I was looking for something much deeper and, yes, personal. That's when I realized that Keanu Reeves was staring me in the face.

He was a good and decent person who, like all good and decent people, had a rollercoaster life. He was a person of humanity and character who just happened to moonlight as a massive celebrity. How he encountered obstacles and made it through them, for better or worse, and examples of just what a good person he was at heart, could be the hook. Using his work as a signpost that lead to his personal struggles and triumphs was the way to go.

And so, *Keanu Reeves's Excellent Adventure: An Unauthorized Biography,* was born.

Pure journalism and the requisite amount of research ensued. As the stories piled up and his triumphs and heartaches found their way to the page, I often found it difficult to be emotionally detached from Reeves. I was, at times, feeling sorry for him, rooting for him, cheering him on, and mentally high fiving him as he moved through his life and his challenges. All pretense of keeping a distance was slowly fading. Whether I liked it or not, I was on his side.

The main hook throughout the writing was that even the hint of cynicism, ego or Hollywood bullshit was nowhere to be found, and believe me I looked. Keanu Reeves was unfolding as a simple, down-to-earth guy making his way through a world of glitz, glamour, rampant egos and big money with quiet confidence and integrity intact.

There was no getting away from the fact that he was something special. But I never had the urge to put him on a pedestal. To make him appear something bigger than the rest of us seemed out of place with who the real Keanu Reeves really was.

And so in *Keanu Reeves's Excellent Adventure: An Unauthorized Biography*, what he is, is decidedly human.

Marc Shapiro, 2020

PREFACE
KEANU NEVER SUCKS

William Irwin is a Professor of Philosophy at Kings College in Wilkes-Barre, Pennsylvania. But if you're looking for the stereotypical college teacher, Irwin is not it. When not in the classroom, the enthusiastic and, by turns, funny Irwin has also moonlighted as the originator of the "philosophy-meets-pop culture" book genre with such bestsellers *as Seinfeld and Philosophy: A Book About Everything and Nothing* and *The Simpsons and Philosophy: The D'oh! of Homer*. In an interview conducted in early June 2020, Irwin took on the burning question of just what makes Keanu Reeves tick.

Irwin is well aware that Keanu has been the topic of a growing interest in academic circles and he's not surprised.

"Contemplating Keanu is a cottage industry. A lot of academics like Keanu because he is so ambiguous, so open to interpretation, a blank canvas on which to paint ideas and apply theories. Keanu is blank, but not vacant. And that's important. We know his ancestry, but his appearance is ethnically androgynous. But he does have feminine qualities. He's certainly no alpha male. There's no toxic masculinity there."

Irwin offers that much of Keanu's popularity stems from a sense of universal love, and that there's much that goes into that feeling.

"He has a distinctive one-word name, 'Keanu', that helps to elevate his iconic status. But Keanu is ultimately loved because he is awesome. I mean that in a technical sense. Awesome people express individuality in a way that invites community. An awesome action creates a social opening. This is the kind of thing that Keanu has done repeatedly. For example, reading aloud to fellow passengers in a van or cuddling with puppies while answering fan questions. The ultimate awesome gesture is the high five, and Keanu would never leave you hanging if you tried to high five him. The opposite of awesome is sucky and Keanu is never sucky. Anyone who would hate on Keanu is sucky!"

The professor delves deeper into Keanu, offering ways in which he stands out from the stereotypical impressions we have of celebrities.

"He seems pleased with success rather than taking it for granted. He's authentic and approachable the way old-school country singers were. This is almost unheard of in Hollywood. Bill Murray, who is very un-Hollywood, is the only other actor who comes to mind. Keanu is not political or preachy. He has his interests and pursuits but he doesn't have airs about him. He does not pretend to be something he is not. He has a quest quality, always searching. He's very Buddha-like."

Given these traits, Irwin admits that on occasion he's been surprised at the actor's sheer complexity.

"I've been pleasantly surprised at the longevity

of his career. I first saw him in 1986 in *River's Edge*, a movie that meant a lot to me as an alienated teenager quite like the one he portrayed. I then saw him in 1988 in *Dangerous Liaisons*. A lot of people didn't like him in that, but I thought he was perfect in the part. His career went on from there with some quiet times when he did smaller movies and had some flops. So I guess I'm surprised that public opinion has finally caught up with my opinion concerning Keanu. I compare this to the song 'Crazy Train,' which only heavy metal fans knew and liked throughout the 1980's. Now everyone knows it and most people like it. Ozzy Osbourne is awesome much like Keanu."

Irwin concedes that Keanu's propensity for being secretive and elusive only adds to his attraction.

"There isn't anything calculated about Keanu. Keanu seems more of a work in progress, going with the flow, the Tao. The most interesting people we know in our personal lives are like this—stable but not rigid, and open to change. We can ask ourselves: What would Keanu do? We don't necessarily know. But we know that he wouldn't be a dick, a jerk or an asshole. If we asked him what to do, he would not have instructions. He'd just say 'dude, be nice.'"

Irwin finally concedes that, in philosophical terms, even Keanu might not really know Keanu.

"Knowing yourself is the great philosophical quest. No one really knows himself or herself. Keanu is in good company here and he maybe better than most at being open to change and self exploration."

Irwin was so taken with the process of getting inside Keanu's head for the purposes of this book that

he was inspired to spontaneously write a poetic ode to
Keanu Reeves.

> Awesome
> Hymn to him
> Who has Keanu cool
> Absorbing insults without offense
> Playing parts without pretension
> Loving people not attention

INTRODUCTION
KARMA KEANU

Going into 2019, Keanu seemed to be on top of the world. He had long since cemented his reputation as box-office royalty and, with new *Bill and Ted*, *Matrix* and *John Wick* movies on the horizon, professionally he had it all. But personally?

Keanu Reeves in love? By November 2019, the answer was that he just might be. Not that this breathless proclamation was anything new. Over the years, Keanu's love life had become a pop culture perennial. It seemed like every time devoted fans turned around, their favorite actor/personality was always seriously with somebody. But this time, the consensus around the world was this just might be the real thing.

Hollywood was abuzz with excitement and anticipation and had the photos to back them up when Reeves, 55, was captured stepping out on the town with longtime friend, business partner, artist and philanthropist Alexandra Grant, 46, at the LACMA Art and Film Gala in Los Angeles.

As observers noted, they were acting very much a couple, holding hands and standing close together as they posed for paparazzi cameras, something the actor had scrupulously avoided doing in close to four decades. But this time Keanu appeared at ease, relaxed and happy as the cameras clicked away. While the ravenous Hollywood press perceived this as their official coming out as a couple by, sharp-eyed journalists were quick to note that a month earlier, Keanu and Alexandra had, in fact, been spotted arriving and leaving a posh Santa Monica, California, restaurant.

But to hear actress Jennifer Tilly tell it in a *Page Six* interview, Keanu and Alexandra have been more than friends for a lot longer than that. "I remember a couple of years ago Grant said 'Keanu Reeves is my boyfriend.' It's really astonishing to me how, in the last five months, all of a sudden she goes to an event with him and everybody goes insane. It's just suddenly surfaced that he's been dating her for several years."

Bottom line, the relationship of everybody's favorite internet boyfriend and perennial Hollywood bachelor was now out in the open. And it wasn't surprising that Keanu was mum on the subject.

On the other hand, after the gossip frenzy settled, Alexandra seemed to have no problem having a good laugh and offering a bit of personal insight into their relationship. In conversation with *Vogue UK,* she said, "I think every single person I knew called me in the first week of November and that's fascinating. Love at every level is deeply important to my identity. I do not believe that isolation is the way. I deeply value the experience of being in relationships."

So, is it true love or just two longtime friends (Reeves and Grant have known each other since 2011) out for a friendly night on the town? Given Reeves' legendary low key and private nature, nobody really knows for sure. His team had long since gotten used to the idea of being mum of their client's personal life, and this time was no exception. And it went without saying that Keanu was not talking.

Completists will tell you that Reeves has been with a lot of women over the years. Not surprisingly. There was just something about the guy that was anti-Hollywood. He was a nice guy, humble, attentive, stoic. What woman would *not* be interested in Keanu?

So sure, he has not been a monk. But research shows that he has not been in a serious relationship since the early 2000's. But it's safe to say that the actor has not been a shrinking violet with the opposite sex during all these years, and has been quick to acknowledge in interviews that, philosophically and spiritually, love and relationships are an important element of his life makeup. So much so, in fact, that entire websites, such as *Goalcast.com* and *Brainy Quote*, have devoted immense amounts of space to Keanu's philosophy of the heart.

"What sort of girls do I like? They are all angels."

"It's fun to be hopelessly in love. It's dangerous but it's fun."

"Falling in love and having a relationship are two different things."

Over the years, Keanu's philosophy of life has been something to behold. He wanders through a celebrity world of ego, greed and, often downright dishonesty a man at peace and balance, while remaning one who rarely conforms. It's a contrariness that Keanu easily and freely talks about.

"I don't live in a mansion," he said in a quote from *PickTheBrain.com*. "I don't have bodyguards. I don't wear fancy clothes. I'm worth $100 million and I still ride the subway."

Being all over the place emotionally and spiritually has long been the mystery and the mystique of Keanu. So while he may be in love or may be *not* in love in November 2019, if karma and decades of good deeds count for anything, he deserves to have true love. Keanu did not come by the title of nice guy by accident. It's something that has been cultivated over the decades via a seemingly endless array of good deeds. To wit…

Keanu once gave a down-on-his-luck set builder on the movie *The Matrix* a $20,000 check as a Christmas bonus. A woman was stranded with a broken-down car on an isolated highway outside of Los Angeles when a black Porsche unexpectedly pulled up beside her. It was Keanu, who attempted to jumpstart her car. Failing that, he called AAA and, in an only-in-Hollywood moment, offered to drive her 50 miles out of his way to make sure she got home. After making sure the woman was safe, Keanu gave her his phone number and told her to call him if she needed further help. The woman would later offer that that he did not put a move on her and had behaved like a true gentleman.

The stories of good-guy Keanu are so numerous and legendary as to have taken on a life of their own and, on the surface, appear too good to be true. But they are.

Keanu once hung out with a homeless man, spending some time—sharing drinks, food and listening to his stories—and, according to passing paparazzi who captured the moment for posterity,

Keanu seemed truly interested in the homeless man and what he had to say.

Keanu had long preferred traveling around town on public transportation and was photographed on one occasion giving up his seat on a bus to a woman. Keanu has traditionally been uncomfortable with many of the perks and privilege of celebrity, preferring to just blend in as part of the crowd. Nowhere was this more evident than one rainy night in Hollywood when he ended up standing out in the downpour for the wrap party for his own film *Daughter of God* before a mix up on the guest list was finally resolved. Those on the scene would marvel at how Keanu could have easily thrown a fit, told the bouncer who he was and pulled the celebrity card. That he did not and came across as a real human being was not surprising. Because Keanu Reeves' reputation as a man of the people had long since been set in stone.

Keanu remains humbled and self- effacing in the onslaught of "nice guy" plaudits and, as acknowledged in a collection of quotes from *PickTheBrain.com*, chalks it up to a good upbringing. Although it would be anything but the stereotypical, white picket fence family situation, Keanu would grow up hardly acknowledging the existence of his biological father and would deal with the emotional rollercoaster of having scattered relationships with his three subsequent stepfathers. But through it all, his Bohemian/hippie mother Patricia taught him the fragments of decency that would be with him always.

"I was raised to treat people exactly how I would like to be treated by others. It's called respect.

"I was taught to knock before I open a door. To say hello when I enter a room. To say please and thank you and to have respect for my elders. I'd let another person have my seat if they needed it. I say yes sir and no sir and help others when they need me and do not stand on the sidelines and watch."

Yes, in this cynical world, Keanu's attitude often sounds too good to be true. But because it weighs out to be true, it's no wonder that fans and hard-eyed observers alike are pulling for him to find true love. A karmic sign that after a whole lot of heartache and struggle, it's time the fates balance the scales because, truth be known, Keanu has not had an easy life.

He's spent a lifetime estranged from his father. He's struggled with dyslexia. Keanu has lost a close friend to a drug overdose. He met the love of his life and lost her to tragedy. He has grieved and has been disappointed, but Keanu has seemingly made it through the challenges in his life unscathed.

"Even in the face of tragedy, a stellar person can thrive," Keanu said philosophically in *PickTheBrain. com*." Life is worth living."

And for Keanu circa 2020, there is still much to reflect and, yes, speculate on. There is a past, present and future to consider. There is a certainty of unexpected personal and professional moves that will only serve to deepen the mystique of a celebrity of massive proportions who moves to the beat of his own drum.

And no one is more aware of that than Keanu himself.

"Most people know me," said Keanu in *PickTheBrain.com*. But they don't know my story."

CHAPTER ONE
BEFORE THERE WAS KEANU

Patricia Taylor was born in 1944 in the city of Hampshire in the United Kingdom. Things get a bit sketchy at that point. Research and a whole lot of speculation indicates that the family tree may have had distant ties to royalty and the generations had roots across the globe. Other notions saw Patricia's parents being very conservative. Who her parents are or what they did seems to have vanished without leaving a trace. What is known about Patricia's childhood is equally sparse.

But what one can sense through the bits and pieces of information was that Patricia, at an early age, was a wild child in the making. She was very much an emotional byproduct of the age, smitten by the notion of creativity, adventure and the great wide world that most certainly existed outside the confines of prim and proper Hampshire. Her spirit was, by all accounts, restless at the notion of experiencing life on a much more expansive level. And so at age 15, Patricia left home and was soon out and about in the world.

Suddenly emancipated, Patricia embraced the concept of truly being on her own and would prove fearless in the face of unknown possibilities. Patricia made her way throughout Europe for the next three years, spending time in Paris and gravitating toward the garish element of show business, acquiring the skills, as both a costume designer and a showgirl, to make her way. By age 19, Patricia had travelled to the Middle East, where she landed a job as a showgirl at a popular Beirut, Lebanon casino.

It was there that she crossed paths with 21-year-old Samuel Nowlin Reeves, a transplanted Hawaiian native who, much like Patricia, was attracted to the "anything goes" lifestyle of the early '60s.

Samuel's parents had divorced when he was 10. His mother remarried and the resultant odyssey around Europe found the young Samuel falling in love with the idea of wanderlust and drugs.

Samuel acknowledged in a *Honolulu Star Bulletin* interview that "I had always smoked pot. In Beirut, I did some cocaine and heroin."

While in Beirut, Samuel worked for a time as a clerk in a publishing house. Stories have circulated over the years that indicated he might have spent some time in a university and also worked as a geologist. But, by his own admission, Samuel told the *Honolulu Star Bulletin* that he "really did not have a trade."

What he did have was an eye for Patricia Taylor.

It was the '60s and it was, for Samuel and Patricia, love and lust at first sight. Without going into details, Samuel admitted to the *Honolulu Star Bulletin* that "She roped me in as soon as I saw her." Samuel was hopelessly hooked and, accordingly, he was open for anything that came of the relationship. "When she got pregnant she flat out told me that 'I'm going to pop out the little buggah so we're getting married.' It was fine with me."

For a short period of time, the couple was quite the item in Beirut, often being spotted, as reported by *Vanity Fair*, driving down the street in their purple Jaguar XKE with Patricia looking very much a child of the '60s in a cowboy hat, blue jeans and a mink coat. On the surface, all was bliss.

But Samuel would, years later, concede that marriage to Patricia was probably not the wisest move as he spoke about in the far-reaching *Honolulu Star Bulletin* interview. "It was the '60s. It was a hard time to be married."

However, Samuel did not duck his responsibilities. The couple married and he remained the dutiful, supportive husband throughout the months of Patricia's pregnancy. Keanu Henry Reeves was born in Beirut, Lebanon on September 2, 1964. The name Keanu was in honor of Samuel's favorite uncle, Henry Keanu Reeves.

A literal translation of Keanu is "Cool breeze over the mountains."

CHAPTER TWO
DADDY ISSUES

By the time Patricia gave birth to the couple's second child, a daughter named Kim, on September 16, 1966, the marriage of Samuel and Patricia was, for all intents and purposes, over. The reasons were many and there seemed be evidence on both sides that neither parent was cut out for a job which revolved around a level of responsibility, commitment and love that neither seemed to possess at that time.

Samuel continued to have issues with both drugs and alcohol throughout the marriage, and was more inclined toward getting into trouble and living recklessly than being an upstanding husband and father. For her part, Patricia continued to crave the spotlight in the rest of the world and, although reportedly a good mother, she chaffed at the limitations of domesticity.

Keanu's childhood years have long been subject to conjecture. The most popular version appears to be, upon further research, inconsistent at best.

Shortly after Kim's birth, Samuel and Patricia moved from Beirut to Toronto, where, according to countless reports, Samuel decided he was finished with the burden of responsibility and abandoned the family. During an interview with the *Honolulu Star Bulletin*,

Samuel attempted to set the record straight. He denied the abandonment charges, offering that during the time he had allegedly walked out, he had been traveling with his brother and earning a living caring for his stepfather's horses. He further acknowledged that Patricia and he had shared the apartment in Toronto until Keanu turned 5 years old.

As with everything else surrounding Keanu's childhood, there appears to be an alternate take on those early years promulgated by his father In a 1996 interview with *TV Week*, Samuel acknowledged the move, but the chronology differed. He offered that the family did relocate from Lebanon, but was quick to correct what he perceived as wrong information.

"We moved from Lebanon to Sydney, Australia because things were getting dangerous in the country because of political and social reasons. There was shootings, shellings and kidnappings all the time. We arrived in Sydney when Keanu was five and my wife Patricia was pregnant with our second child Kim."

Samuel related to *TV Week* that Sydney, by contrast, was a breath of fresh air, a warm and inviting place that seemed to smooth over the seemingly rough patches in Samuel and Patricia's relationship. Samuel found work in a film lab and spent quality time with his entire family, especially Keanu. "The years we spent in Australia were the happiest of Keanu's childhood. I would teach him to swim and we would always ride together on my motorcycle."

This is where Keanu's early childhood odyssey appears to dovetail around to the family leaving Australia for Canada and the inevitable dissolution of the Reeves' marriage. A cousin, Leslie Reeves, in a candid conversation excerpted in *Vanity Fair*, saw the end coming. "There were always fights about Sam's drug taking. My aunt grew out of the hippie phase. My uncle refused. In fact, he wouldn't give up the drugs."

Although there was the occasional story that indicated that Samuel and Patricia would remain legally married until Keanu turned 15, the consensus was that the couple officially divorced in 1966 when Samuel walked out on the family and into decades of drug-infused misadventures.

How Keanu took his father walking out on him has seemingly left an indelible psychological scar that, in later years, he would avoid dealing with, but, in recent times, he would face, on occasion, be candid in talking about.

"The story of me and my father is pretty heavy stuff," Keanu was quoted in *US Magazine*. "I knew him up until I was six, then I would see him on occasion when I would visit him in Hawaii on holidays. He recalled that the last time he saw his father, at age 13, was an existential exercise as he explained in an *US Magazine* interview. "We were in Kauai and I remember my father speaking about the stars, something about how the world is a box. I had no idea what he was talking about. But I remember he was speaking about the stars as we looked up."

Years later Keanu would recall his final moments with his father in a *Penthouse Magazine* interview. He said that his father "brought my sister and I to the airport and that was it. We didn't hear anything from him for 10 years. No calls. No letters. No nothing."

At that point, Keanu was emotionally spent on the subject of his father. But, by the mid-'90's, the absence of a father in his life had seemingly taken a psychological and emotional toll. A sense of anger began to surface, an anger born of frustration and loss, the young actor exploded in a mid-'90s interview chronicled in *TV Week*.

"My father is nothing but a 60's deadbeat reject."

The anger and loss would continue to fester over the years. As late as 2017, in a *Rolling Stone* conversation, Keanu found it difficult to control his ire at yet another question about the relationship with his father.

"The story with me and my dad is pretty heavy. It's full of pain and woe and a fucking loss and all that shit."

A year later, January 26, 2018, Samuel passed away. To the end, Samuel would constantly make attempts through family members and the media to try and reconnect with his son. But Keanu would not acknowledge those attempts, and, on the day of the funeral, Keanu did not attend.

CHAPTER THREE
WILD LIFE

Following the disillusion of her marriage to Samuel, Patricia would juggle duties as a single mother while attempting to carve out a living in what had become her chosen profession as a costume designer. She would prove to be quietly aggressive when it came to her chosen profession, showcasing determination and confidence, in an entertainment world that often continued to look askance at a woman attempting to better herself. It would come as no surprise that Patricia would soon be going places.

And then there was the other side of her, one of surprising tradition. As an English woman, Patricia was well versed in the world of manners and respect, two qualities that she passed down to her children when they were quite young. But she quickly found that Toronto, at least during a brief first stay that went largely unnoticed, was not the place to establish herself professionally.

Keanu suggested as much during an interview with *Penthouse* in which he disclosed that Patricia loved Toronto but ultimately decided that New York, professionally, was where she had to be. "My mother despised New York but New York was where she was able to work in her profession and support us all."

Patricia arrived in New York and immediately embraced the thrills, excitement and possibilities of The Great White Way. For Keanu and Kim, their introduction into their mother's world was a surreal landscape of hotels and the seemingly endless round of meeting interesting and colorful people. Their time in New York was also eye-opening for Patricia. Her skills as a costume designer were slowly but surely accepted in the'60s outrageousness and experimentation in style and lifestyle. It all fed Patricia's spontaneity and impulsiveness. Especially when it came to affairs of the heart...

Romance arrives in the guise of Broadway and film producer Paul Aaron. Aaron was a comer in New York, a deft creative mind with style, intellect and, according to those who knew him well, he possessed a sly sense of humor. He was making his mark on the New York stage in the late '60s and early '70s with alternately intriguing and intoxicating productions of *Salvation*, *Paris Is Out*, *A Dream Is Out* and *70 Girls 70*.

The attraction between Taylor and Aaron was immediate, and the relationship progressed at lightspeed. By September 1970 they were married.

The couple decided that it would be easier to raise the family far from the hectic environment of New York City, and moved back to Toronto. Ever the pragmatist, Patricia saw the move to Toronto as a way to be closer to her ex-in-laws, who had stayed friends with her through the divorce from Samuel, and who had offered to help support the family until Patricia's career took off.

For his part, Keanu found Toronto and, particularly the town of Yorkville an idyllic place to grow up in during his early childhood years. During a *Redditt* interview he fondly recalled that he loved going to a hamburger stand called Licks and hanging out in Ramsden Park. He recalled in a *Total Film* conversation that "Yorkville these days is pretty high-end but when I was this young street kid there were strip clubs all over the place and a great candy store/head shop called *The Grab Bag* and The Bloor Street Cinema, where I saw a whole lot of movies."

For a very short period of time the marriage seemed to work. The entire family adopted Canadian citizenship and, for a time, according to Kim Reeves in a *People Magazine* story, the children adopted many of Aaron's Jewish religious traditions. "When mom was married to Paul, we dressed in white every Friday night and sang Shabbat songs. In the summer, we would go to Jewish camps."

By March 1971, they were divorced. The reason has never been fully explained, so observers are left to ponder a relationship that was all too much and too fast. More than one report indicated that it was Paul who left the family (a patten of parental abandonment that was quickly making itself a part of Keanu's psyche). But by all accounts, the divorce was amicable. So much so that Keanu formed an immediate and solid friendship with Aaron.

The divorce of Patricia and Paul would coincide with sudden resurgence in her career as a costume designer, especially as it pertained to the rock music community. Keanu and his sister's early years would be marked by large doses of the rock life as the likes of David Bowie, Alice Cooper and Dolly Parton would drift in and out of Patricia's home studio as she sat at her sewing machine, creating wildly extravagant costumes for the performers.

"I grew up on this street called Hazelton in Toronto," he reflected in a *Toronto Sun* conversation, "and I mingled with a lot of stars when I was a youngster. My mother was into costume design, she was into rock and roll, she was in the business and she had friends."

Keanu recalled those days with fondness in an interview with *Penthouse*. "My mother loved music. When she sat at her sewing machine there was always some kind of record spinning in the background. Our little brick house turned into a pass through house for glam rockers who wanted to look good on their tours. Alice Cooper was always around and ready for some kind of joke. He would do things like put fake vomit and fake dog shit on our sofa to drive our cleaning lady crazy. My home turned into a giant playground in which even the adults played."

Keanu related in the *Toronto Sun* that Cooper was a close friend and so trusted that Patricia would occasionally leave Cooper to babysit Keanu and Kim while she was off doing business. "Alice Cooper would babysit us when I was very young," Keanu revealed to *The Toronto Sun*. "I don't remember a lot but I do remember that when he was babysitting us, there was always some disgusting stuff like fake poo in the refrigerator or hidden around the house. So in that way it connected to me that Alice had been taking care of us."

That Patricia would trust her young children with, for that time, the most notorious shock rocker on the planet, was a clue as to Patricia's approach to parenting. The young mother was still a free-spirited bohemian at heart and would not think twice about going off and leaving her children to, literally and figuratively, fend for themselves.

Years later, Keanu would express the somewhat harsh put-down of his mother in more diplomatic terms in a conversation with *Dolly Magazine*. "My mom once told me that after the word 'no,' the second thing I spoke was 'how come?' It drove her crazy. But she encouraged that openness in me. Our life was long on love beads, incense and visits from her clients but short on discipline."

Keanu was equally candid, years later, when discussing his mother's parenting skills with *Esquire* magazine. "We were latchkey kids. It was basically leave the house in the morning and come back at night. But even for a runaway English girl, my mother gave us a proper upbringing. We learned manners, respect for our elders and formal table settings."

Likewise, Patricia, looking back on those wild and wooly days with *TV Park*, was her own best and worst critique on the subject. "I didn't raise my children. I just watched them grow."

The growth process for Keanu and, to a lesser degree, Kim, was nothing if not chaotic. Both children had been diagnosed with dyslexia at an early age. The ailment, essentially an aversion to comprehending words and, by association, books, contributed to a growing sense of insecurity and isolation that was particularly evident in Keanu, whose young psyche would continue to be rattled by his mother's constantly moving in and out of relationships and marriages, her seeming lack of orthodox parental guidance, and the idea of isolation and insecurity that Keanu cultivated early on.

He made friends easily, but often seemed to keep those friendships at an emotional distance. By the time he entered kindergarten at Toronto's Jesse Ketchum Public School System, where he would continue until grade eight, he was mentally and emotionally living in his own world. And his teachers would be the first to notice.

Paula Wardner, one of Keanu's teachers during his years at Jesse Ketchum, recalled her less-than-prize student during a conversation with *People*. "I don't think Keanu ever got to class on time and, when he did arrive, he wasn't quite with it. He always left his books at home or forgot his homework. But he'd just smile and go back and get them. And somehow he did manage to pass his classes."

Keanu did not agree with Wardner's assessment during an interview with *Her Moments.com*. "I don't remember having trouble fitting in. I kind of blended in."

In fact, he blended to the point where he soon became part and parcel of the ritual of school life. He would hang out, make friends and, in due course, become involved in schoolyard scuffles. "I think grade school was the last time I was really fighting," he recalled to *The Daily Beast*. "There were fights and I would end up in the principals' office. It would just happen once in a while. I remember there was one time I was actually winning a fight and then I thought 'Well you don't really need to fight.' So I just stopped fighting. It was like 'Cool, man… let's just stop fighting."

Despite his spotty academic record, Keanu would consider Jesse Ketchum a bright spot. "Jesse Ketchum was such a non-protected, open-to-the world learning environment, socially," he offered in a *Globe and Mail* interview. "It was a great cross section of kids from first grade to eighth grade. It was the best of what you would think of as a liberal education."

During this time, acting was the furthest thing from the young boy's mind. But, at age 9, he stumbled into his first official theatrical gig when, while at summer camp, he appeared in the chorus of a production of *Damned Yankees*. Little remains of that experience; even Keanu himself remembers little save for the fact that he did it.

As he prepared to graduate from the eighth grade, there was a sense of disillusionment surrounding Keanu's academic potential. Not surprisingly, there were pockets of support which came primarily from the young underachiever's mother. Patricia insisted that her son was intellectually superior and was capable of handling the requirements of an advanced institution. And so...

"When I got out of grade eight I picked the best academic school, even though I wasn't a very good student," Keanu reflected in an *US* interview. "I was the only one from Jesse Ketchum who went there so that was sort of weird."

CHAPTER FOUR
KEANU ACTS OUT

"Weird" would turn out to be Avondale Secondary Alternative School, and for Keanu, it would be the beginning of a five-year odyssey through four high schools that would also include De La Salle College, Etobicoke School of the Arts and the Toronto School of Performing Arts. The changes would leave Keanu emotionally dazed and confused.

There was a lot of baggage as Keanu entered the cycle of Canadian high schools. The young boy was constantly on a rollercoaster of family dysfunction thanks, in no small part, to his mother Patricia, who continued to live and work in a bohemian, rock and roll lifestyle that was big on freedom and short on family structure and rules.

The Reeves children continued to ride the waves of a freeform family life. Their mother would often have to go out of town on business, leaving them with a nanny, but largely on their own. The likes of David Bowie, Dolly Parton and Emmylou Harris were always in and out and, on more than one occasion, Keanu would witness the excess and debauchery of the rock and roll lifestyle. Left to his own devices, Keanu would find relatively normal pursuits; a paper route and afternoons at the local second-run movie theater where he would spend afternoons watching Bruce Lee movies.

Midway through Keanu's high school years, Patricia married rock music promoter Robert Miller, a union that would produce a half-sister for Keanu, adding more fodder to his complex life.

A big part of Keanu's failure to find footing in higher education stemmed from the nomadic nature of Patricia Taylor's life. The family was seemingly always on the move to a new home, and it would be something that Keanu would, in later years, confess to being an issue for him. In conversation with *Choices Magazine*, he said, "It's difficult constantly being uprooted and changing your environment. It's hard moving to new places, making new friends and leaving behind your old environment. I wouldn't say it was the most traumatizing experience, but it sure seemed like it back then."

And then there was his dyslexia, which continued to manifest itself in inconsistent behavior, especially when it came to the requirements of a high school education. "High school was difficult," Keanu would understate in conversations with *The Daily Mail* and *Dyslexia Help.com*. "I often pretended to understand school as a way of coping with the fact that I didn't fit in."

Nor did he seem to try.

Beginning with one-year stops at Avondale Secondary Alternative School and Etobicoke School of the Arts, the perception of Keanu as student outcast was cemented in the minds of both instructors and fellow students. By his own estimation Keanu was rambunctious, wild and mouthy.

"I was greasy and running around a lot," Keanu reflected about his early high school days in an interview with *US*. "I was just a little too rambunctious and shot my mouth off a little too often. I was not generally the most well-oiled machine in school. I was just getting in everybody's way I guess."

But Keanu would insist that, despite his bad behavior, academically he did have his moments at those schools. "I guess I was okay academically," he recalled in a *Daily Mail* conversation. "I was good at English and creative writing and I was on the chess team." But it would be his basic disinterest, coupled with poor grades and attendance, that finally ended his tenure at Etobicoke School of The Arts.

However, Keanu continued to give formal education a try. But by the time he arrived at his third high school, De La Salle College, even the ever-optimistic Keanu had to admit that he was on a downward spiral, as explained to *The Express On Sunday Magazine*. "I failed every class except Latin. Latin was the only class I liked. My attendance record was very bad. I was lazy and school wasn't important to me."

Except when it came to sports. In his own rather unorthodox way, Keanu was quite the athlete in both ice hockey and, to a lesser degree, soccer. But as he would concede in a *Handbag.com* interview that hockey was both a physical and therapeutic pastime. "I was always pretty shy and I didn't really feel confident unless I was on the ice. Hockey allowed me to be something different. The rest of the time was just goofing off and hanging out."

On the ice, Keanu quickly acquired quite the reputation as a goalie who could stop any puck and, accordingly, carried the nickname of "The Wall" through his time at De La Salle. As the Most Valuable

Player awards piled up, Keanu began to dream of a berth on the Canadian Olympic Team and the very real possibility of turning professional. Unfortunately, an injury would curtail his hockey aspirations.

Keanu would continue to keep in contact with his ex-stepfather Paul Aaron who, following his divorce from his mother, had relocated to Southern California for work. During school vacations, the youngster would often go visit Aaron in Hollywood and hang out on the sets of whatever production Aaron was working on. Consequently, Keanu saw how the magic was made, and was fascinated by the idea of actors and what they went through in the name of their craft. In his mind, the fantasy and reality of being an actor was now firmly.

Once again aimless and basically going through the motions at De La Salle, Keanu enrolled in yet another high school, the Toronto School Of The Performing Arts. It was not an easy school to get into, requiring a battery of interviews and finally, an audition. Nobody was more surprised than Keanu when he passed his audition. It would be a pivotal moment in which the idea of acting, only a fleeting notion since his summer camp debut in *Damn Yankees* but a subtle form of encouragement from ex-stepfather Paul Aaron, suddenly took flight.

Aaron recalled the transformation he saw in his former stepson during an interview with Canadian magazine *MacLeans*. "Like everything else he does, that (acting) became his sole abiding interest. I mean every part of it, the voice, the movement, the contemporary, the classical."

For a time, Keanu seemed enthusiastic about school. Reportedly, his grades were passable, and the lure of acting, most notably in a production of *The Crucible*, had, by degrees, made him a reasonably competent student. Keanu found the role of Mercutio in a high school production of *Romeo & Juliet* to be particularly enticing. In *Interview* magazine, he enthused "Mercutio in *Romeo & Juliet* was so full of passion and wisdom and anger."

There was something about the acting process and creating memorable roles and characters that was serious business, and he gravitated toward it with a drive that he had not felt before. And it was that unexpected drive that immediately put Keanu at odds with his fellow students. Keanu had risen to heights as an actor and, in his opinion, his fellow students were not serious enough about the craft. There would be constant clashes of ego, but there were few who could argue that Keanu had suddenly found acting as his mental and emotional breakthrough. Those privy to those early performances would marvel at how the teenager who was normally distracted to the max could suddenly take on a role and immerse himself in it to the exclusion of anything else. Admittedly, Keanu was a raw student at that point, but he was also displaying a real sense of soul.

It was during this year at Toronto School of The Arts that Keanu had his first legitimate bit of notoriety as a roving reporter on the Canadian Broadcast Network's reality series *Going Great*, a program dedicated to the amazing achievements of young people. Keanu's job was to interview the show's young guests with questions that ranged from softball to obvious. Keanu would later show real embarrassment when long-lost clips of the show would be dredged up on the talk show circuit, and would concede that he was often awkward in the extreme when conducting interviews. *Going Great* would last two seasons. Keanu was let go after season one.

Through it all, Keanu was still Keanu, and the result was that his behavior and defiance of authority continued. Keanu recounted the inevitable decline at Toronto School of The Arts to a *Daily Mail* reporter. "I got into a performing arts school but I didn't fit in. I had conflicts and run-ins with the staff and the principal and I didn't see eye to eye with any of them. I was one of those 'why' kids. I asked too many questions about everything."

It would be that constant nattering between Keanu and the staff of Toronto School of The Arts that finally produced a major blow up and the proverbial last straw. In a detailed article in *People*, the exchange between Keanu and an instructor went like this. After a heated back and forth between Keanu and a teacher, the instructor admonished his pupil that, "He would just have to bite the bullet." To which Keanu replied, "Yeah, but I don't have to eat the whole rifle."

Consequently, less than a year after enrolling at Toronto School of The Arts and shortly after turning 16, Keanu was expelled from the institution. The bad news came in the form of an official letter from the school that Keanu recalled in conversation with the *Daily Mail*. His dismissal was said to be due to his inability to concentrate and the fact that he asked too many questions. Bottom line, they saw no future for Keanu as a professional actor or, for that matter, much of a future in any aspect of his life.

"It was a terrible letter to receive, saying you can't come back to school next year. Getting asked to leave was very upsetting."

CHAPTER FIVE
KEANU A.K.A.
PASTAMAN AND WOLFBOY

The upset over his school expulsion was quickly offset by the discovery of Keanu's true calling. He had decided that acting was the thing to pursue. It was just that Keanu was not sure exactly *how* to pursue it. "I jumped into acting without an ultimate goal," he admitted in the book *The New Breed of Actors Coming of Age*. "Later I would realize that if I didn't have any goals, people were going to fuck with me."

Keanu's goal at that point was vague. He was dealing with a tug of war between the reality and the fantasy of it all and it was making his next movie difficult. He knew he wanted to make it as an actor. But he was not sure how to go about it. And so 1983 saw him embarking on a guerilla approach to getting noticed. "I was just trying to live my life," he explained *The New Breed of Actors Coming of Age*. "I started taking acting lessons at night and learning various forms of method acting and sense memory. Then I started crashing local auditions and getting some jobs. Then I joined a community theater group."

It was his early theater experience, which he did

for essentially no pay, that made an impact on Keanu. "The theater can actually do something that's physical, emotional and human," Keanu explained in a quote credited to *Dell Publishing* and archived in the Keanu Reeves website *whoaisnotme.net*

The year 1983 would prove eventful. He had heard that the Leah Polsun Theatre Company had a sterling reputation for turning out professional actors. He auditioned at the prestigious company, and the results of that audition, according to observers, was all over the place.

In a *MacLeans* magazine article, company director Rose Dublin described Keanu as a disheveled mess on his audition day—torn jeans, old sweats, untied running shoes and hair combed over one side of his face. But that initial impression disappeared when Keanu launched into his audition, which included a Shakespeare soliloquy. "We sat there and he just blew us away," Dublin recalled in *MacLeans*. "He had such energy; goofy and sort of macho and uncertain, kind of on the threshold of growing up but not quite there."

In his own very unorthodox, very off-kilter way, Keanu had taken an all-important first step.

During his tenure at Leah Polsun, faculty and fellow actors saw Keanu as a Jekyll and Hyde, alternately distracted and possessed of an extremely short attention span but also, by turn, driven by a passion for acting. The latter state was regularly on display in company productions. In the book *Keanu*, Dublin had particular praise for his performance in *Romeo & Juliet*. "For his age, he was a brilliant Mercutio. He was very exciting to watch. We sat there and wondered how someone that young could do such a super job. He had such a range of emotions, comedy, despair, and cynicism. Possibly, it was all the things that Keanu was going through himself."

It was during a production of the play *For Adults Only* that Keanu caught the attention of agent Tracy Moore who, like others, sensed a certain something about the young actor and signed him immediately. In the book *Keanu*, Moore recalled that she sent her client out for just about everything, just to get his feet wet. "And every time he went out, he seemed to get something. He was a sure sell in a way. He was always extremely intense. He took his work very seriously. He had a direction in his head and he went for it."

Although his marriage to Keanu's mother did not survive, Paul Aaron remained a behind-the-scenes guardian angel for his former stepson, offering advice and lending an ear during Keanu's early days as a struggling actor. In one instance he pulled some professional strings when he recommended his Keanu to a position at the prestigious Hedgerow Theater, a professional acting company in Pennsylvania. Keanu took up the offer, spending that first summer on his own sweeping floors and doing all manner of manual labor at the company in exchange for extensive acting and drama instruction. After that summer at Hedgerow, he returned to Toronto with a new sense of seriousness about his chosen profession.

His time at the Hedgerow once again whet Keanu's appetite for the stage and playing Shakespearian greats, and he attempted to join a pair of Shakespearian regional companies. "I wanted to be in the Shaw and Shakespeare Festivals," he told *The Los Angeles Times*, "but they turned me down twice. I didn't fit. I was too young and unruly by their standards."

But it was during his Leah Polsun period that Keanu began to emerge.

His growing reputation as a good-looking albeit unorthodox actor caught the attention of a casting director for a part in a Coca-Cola commercial. It was a paying gig the likes that Keanu had never seen, a Coke commercial with a heartwarming relationship between father and son, centered around the world of cycling. For that commercial, Keanu was very much in the "method-acting" mode, so much so that he voluntarily shaved his legs to fit the bike-riding image.

Keanu had fond memories of that "big break" during an appearance of *The Late Show with James Cordon*. "I played a cyclist and my dad was my coach and the story revolved around this big race. It was a three-day shoot. It was a great experience because I was going from school to study to the real world. It was all about hitting marks and improvisation."

According to reports it was also about a $4,000 payday, which was more money than Keanu had seen in his life. But rather than blow it, a trait sprang up that would follow him throughout his life: He was matter of fact and smart about money. Rather than open a checking account, Keanu cashed the check and used the money to pay his day-to-day expenses. It was a move that allowed the young actor to continue to develop his craft.

Keanu also made time to have some semblance of an active social life.

He would celebrate his 17th birthday by buying his first car. "It was a 69 Volvo, British racing green," Keanu told *Dolly*. "Bricks held up the front seat. Good stereo. I bought it from a man who ripped me off.

Friends were always having to help me jump start it I remember being with some friends, driving in that car from Toronto, Canada to Buffalo, New York to see The Ramones. There was a punk rock girl in the backseat with a racoon on her shoulder. The Clash were playing so loud on the stereo. And there were all those questions running through my head. Will we make it? We're underage, can we get in? It was an adventure and it was one big good time."

By the time he turned 17, Keanu was the prototypical bohemian/actor on the rise. Shuttling back and forth between his mother's house and, for a time, the basement of a girlfriend's home, he held such exotic jobs as sharpening ice skates, as well as making up to 100 pounds of pasta a day at a tiny restaurant called Pastissima. Keanu became quite good at the pasta game and was eventually promoted to the position of manager. When an audition came up, Keanu would simply close the restaurant.

Reeves' career was progressing at a steady pace into 1984. He landed small roles in the Canadian sitcom *Hangin' In*, the TV movie *Letting Go*, and somewhat bigger roles in smaller films like *One Step Away*.

Much of his work during this period was obvious and, by degrees, stereotypical. He was the troubled teen, the sidekick, the aimable stoner and, in two episodes of the television series *Night Heat,* he was both a mugger and what was described in final credits as Thug #1, a title Keanu would jokingly claim years later that resulted from his being taller than the actor who ended up playing Thug # 2.

Keanu remembered the growing pains during that period, especially the very early below-the-line roles,

in the book *The New Breed of Actors Coming of Age.*
"*Hangin' In* was a godsend for young actors in
Toronto. They gave lots of roles out to young kids. I
played a tough street kid. I wore stupid clothes and had
no idea what I was doing."

Keanu was still very much a work in progress.

His agent Tracy Moore made no bones about that
fact in the book *Keanu: "At* times he drove me crazy,"
she said, while recalling in a *MacLeans* interview,
Keanu could be headstrong and less than professional,
often showing up for auditions in obvious need of a
shower, wearing ragged shorts and, most grating to
Moore, a pair of beat-up work boots that rarely left his
feet. "The guy wore work boots all the time. We didn't
want him to be remembered as a sloppy, smelly kid,"
Moore remembers. "But his attitude was that didn't
have anything to do with acting ability."

But Keanu, with admittedly more ego and self-
absorption than professional sense, continued to rub
the acting community the wrong way. Keanu's people
were constantly fielding complaints from producers
and directors about how he would regularly be late to
the set and was often at odds with directors. Another
of his agents, Lisa Burke, recalled in a *MacLeans*
interview how his agents sat their young charge down
at one point and had "the talk." "We told him he either
had to shape up or ship out. He began to realize that he
loved this business and started taking it seriously."

Warts and all, Keanu had nevertheless morphed into
a legitimate working actor by the time he had reached 19.
But it would take his appearance in the 1984 stage
production of *Wolfboy* to initially get him into the public
eye. *Wolfboy*, directed by John Palmer from a play by

Brad Fraser, was typical of the way off-Broadway experimental theater that was abroad in the '80s. The story is about an innocent boy placed in a psychiatric institution, where he falls under the influence of a disturbed boy who, at one point in the story, sucks blood from him. *Wolfboy*, with equal elements of vampire conquest and homoerotic overtones, was risky business, as was director John Palmer's approach to casting it.

"I didn't want professional actors so I advertised in the personals (newspaper ads)," Palmer told *Vanity Fair*. "What I got was totally fucked up losers." Among those "losers" was Keanu, whose audition, according to Palmer's memories in *MacLeans,* was "Ludicrous. I mean he had no technique and no training. He couldn't handle two consecutive sentences." But the director saw something else that stood out during that very bad audition. "He had an energy and a glow about him."

Those qualities overcame Keanu's lack of perceived talent and polish, and the teenager soon found himself in rehearsals at the Toronto Theatre Passe Muraille. As the play evolved, Keanu was alternately nervous and a bit giddy about some of the more overt elements of the play. One of the more provocative was a sequence in which Keanu's character, after being sprayed down with water to simulate sweat, had to do pushups while wearing only shorts. For promotional purposes, a poster was shot of Keanu and fellow actor Carl Marotte in a passionate, erotically charged embrace. Keanu had no problem with the fact that *Wolfboy* was being targeted, to a large extent, to the gay community. All he knew was that it was an acting job and that he was going to make the most of it.

Keanu described his experience in *Wolfboy* in

graphic detail in book *The New Breed: Actors Coming of Age*. "There's this guy who thinks he's a wolf who fucks with me and eventually we fall in love. In the last scene of the play he stabs me, the lights go down and I'm laying on the stage with tons of blood all over me and this guy is hunched over me, slurping blood off my chest and licking my mouth. The first couple of shows all these leather boys came. For me that was funny but also scary because, for that first week, I was pretty bad. I got better though and by the end of it (the run of the play) I was pretty rad, thrashing cool."

By the time Keanu turned 20, he found himself at a career standstill. *Wolfboy* had provided his first taste of real notoriety. He was working fairly regularly and always auditioning for something. However, Keanu had also found himself in the midst of stereotyping. Keanu had always envisioned his career leading down the road to being a star, but he had to admit that it wasn't happening. "I was tired of playing the best friend, thug #1 and the tall guy," he lamented in *USA Today*. "There was no room for me as an actor in Canada."

But fate would step in. He was auditioning for a Disney Movie of the Week called *Young Again* (in which he would be credited as K.C. Reeves). Nobody thought much of his audition except the film's director, Steven Hilliard Stern, who not only cast him in the film but used his connections in the States to play him up to agent Hildy Gottlieb at the prestigious ICM Talent Agency. Gottleib was duly impressed and requested that Keanu comes to Los Angeles to take a meeting. The meeting went well and the result was that Keanu was able to get the coveted green card that would allow him to work in the States.

Now his future was up to him. He could stay in Canada and ride out regular work in a limited market with few prospects. Or he could roll the dice.

"With the green card I had the opportunity to go to Los Angeles," he would reflect in *USA Today*. "It was a pretty scary thing but I had to go."

He had cobbled together $3,000 as seed money and convinced his girlfriend at the time that she should tag along; that it would be fun. Family and friends wished him luck and secretly hoped for the best. The aspiring star would chronicle the beginning of the odyssey in typical Keanu fashion, as he related to *Girlfriend Magazine*. "So I get in my car (his '69 Volvo continuing to hang on by a wing and a prayer), pick up my girlfriend and we drive off for Hollywood."

Days later, Keanu arrived at the Hollywood city limits. It was a cathartic moment. He knew this was where he was supposed to be.

Unfortunately, the relationship with his girlfriend and his beloved vehicle did not survive the journey and resultant change of life. Both quickly disappeared into the rest of their lives and the junkyard. As Keanu would lament in *Girlfriend Magazine*, it was all for the best: "I just didn't want that much baggage right now."

CHAPTER SIX
KEANU IN LA LA LAND

Keanu's first thoughts upon arriving in Los Angeles in 1984 were rife with extreme uncertainty. He would often describe the experience, as well as the uneasiness of literally being washed up on a foreign shore, as going into the darkness that was Los Angeles. He described the experience to a *Gannett News Service* reporter more succinctly: "I arrived cold. I didn't have a clue."

Fortunately, Paul Aaron continued to pave the way. By the time Keanu arrived in Hollywood, Aaron had not only used his influence to land his—former stepson both a manager and an agent, but he also told Keanu that he could live with him until he got his bearings. It all seemed good. But Keanu had barely hit the city limits when he got his first taste of how Hollywood worked.

"So I get there (Hollywood) and my manger and agent say 'it's great to see you but we have to change your name," Keanu recalled during an interview with late night television talk show host *Jimmy Fallon.* "They did it the first day I got into town."

The reason offered was that Keanu was too ethnic sounding, and he needed a name that sounded white. They said they would leave it up to Keanu to come up with a new name. That may have been a mistake. With his bullshit meter on high, Keanu came up with the name Chuck Spandin. Manager and agent were not thrilled. His next nom de plume, Templeton Page Taylor, also failed to excite anybody. Finally, Keanu's reps threw in the towel and Keanu remained Keanu.

The newcomer would quickly discover that being a struggling actor in Hollywood could be a lonely existence. Shy by nature, Keanu was slow to make friends and even slower to make his mark. Despite having management and agency representation, Keanu could not land even the smallest of acting roles in his first eight months in town. He was extremely discouraged and, according to several reports, returned to Canada for a time, fully intending to make a go of it as an actor in Toronto, where he had already achieved a small measure of success. But with the encouragement of his former stepfather and the realization that success in Hollywood did not happen overnight, Keanu returned to Hollywood. His determination would be rewarded, albeit with baby steps.

One Step Away (1985) saw Keanu as tormented youth. *Youngblood* (1986) was a hockey film with Keanu playing to type as a hockey goalie. The latter film would go on to have the reputation of being both good and bad, and allow Keanu a firsthand opportunity to see one of his co-stars, Rob Lowe, likewise. Keanu and Lowe got along well enough during the making of *Youngblood* and they hung out together for a time after making the film. It was then that Keanu, as he offered in *Young Americans.com*, saw Lowe's true colors. "We hung out for a while but all he did was try and steal my girlfriends. He almost had his wicked way with two of them but, eventually, they saw through him."

Flying (1986) cast Keanu as the supportive boyfriend in feel-good sports epic. *Acts Of Vengeance* (1986) was a Charles Bronson get-even TV movie, featuring. Keanu as way-below-the-credit-line as a heavy. *Brotherhood of Justice* (1986) found Keanu as vigilante who sees the error of his ways.

Finally, *Babes in Toyland* (1986). It was a three-hour Christmas TV special in which Keanu plays Jack B Nimble. And thus began his first real Hollywood romance with co-star Jill Schoelen, who played the character of Mary Contrary.

Working together on *Babes in Toyland*, it seemed almost inevitable that sparks might fly. Schoelen said as much in conversation with *Obnoxious & Anonymous. com.* "I rarely dated because I was always too busy working. All my boyfriends I met through work." This being years before *TMZ* and the prying eyes of social media, it was not considered a big deal when Keanu and Schoelen embarked in an on-set romance that would continue on after the completion of *Babes In Toyland,* and would ultimately last until 1989.

From the outset, Keanu was not big on talking about his personal life, so it's not surprising that he never spoke publicly about their three-year relationship. As for Schoelen, she dismissed the notion of any personal revelations when she told *Obnoxious & Anonymous.com* "No one really cared when Keanu and I were together."

But there was more than a bit of speculation surrounding the end of their relationship. While the consensus was that the break up was amicable, there were numerous reports that Schoelen broke up with Keanu shortly after being introduced to another struggling actor named Brad Pitt.

Keanu continued to work non-stop throughout 1986. Although most of the roles and projects would be fairly insignificant and fleeting, his star was beginning a slow but steady ascension into the public view. That he was out there getting work brought no small sense of joy to Aaron and, as Keanu offered in *USA Today*, his mother. "She's happy that I'm doing something and that I'm not a bum. There were days where she thought I was going to become part of the couch."

Keanu acknowledged that those early roles were more therapeutic than anything else simply by the fact that he was busy. "Acting is the only thing that keeps me still," he acknowledged at that time to *USA Today*. "If I'm not acting, I bounce off the walls."

Keanu was hardly a social butterfly when not acting. He would occasionally be spotted at dance clubs, but otherwise he projected a reclusive image. His trademark long hair, T-shirt and jeans, coupled with the admission that, at this point, he was only bathing a couple of times a week, lent an air of the outsider to the perceived image of the actor. It wasn't necessarily a bad look professionally, especially at a time when actors were presenting a hardened, anti-establishment persona to the world. When not working, he truly was very much in hiding with esoteric music and books as company.

By the end of 1986, Keanu and the concept of loneliness had begun its march toward becoming an ongoing obsession for both fans and journalists. Just about everybody who had been around Keanu for any length of time would willingly step forward to corroborate that fact during the coming years of increasing fame.

Actor Shia La Beouf, who would work with

Keanu on the movie *Constantine*, said, with tongue firmly planted in cheek, "I don't think he hangs out with other humans that much." Likewise Dennis Hopper, who co-starred with Keanu in *Speed*, added to the lonely Keanu line when he told *BB* that "He could be charming but I think he would be happier if he could get away from people."

As the years have gone by, Keanu, who was notorious for not sharing personal tidbits, would occasionally address the loneliness issue. "I'm trying not to be alone so much," he told *Izismile.com*, "and man, it's a struggle." It would be in conversation with *Star 2.com* that Keanu basically drew the picture of what he was like back in 1986.

"I'm an introvert and a boring kind of person."

CHAPTER SEVEN
SEE KEANU PLAY

"There are no plans," Keanu told *Empire Magazine*. "I find plans. You can have a wish or a desire or a want or a hope."

This bit of philosophical jibber-jabber was part and parcel of Keanu's mindset during his early days in Hollywood. His thoughts and ideas were all over the place and it showed in the often surreal nature of his responses to reporter's questions, which were occasionally serious and insightful, but more often than not, flighty, mocking and self-deprecating. Hollywood soon latched onto the perception that Keanu was perhaps putting them on by playing stupid. It was not necessarily the impression that an up-and-coming actor wanted to present to Hollywood tastemakers. Keanu did his best to reject the "stupid" tag when he looked back on those days for a *Vanity Fair* profile. "I don't play stupid. Either it's been a failure on my part to articulate or my naivete."

Keanu, trying to both establish and find himself, was running up against the wall of an industry that often seemed clueless as to what to do with him. In the movie industry's eyes, Keanu was straddling that line between clichéd teen roles and the potential he was showing for more serious stuff. And going into the late '80s, Keanu was, quite simply, through sage advice and his own youthful intuition, going along for the ride.

What he was not expecting was that a low-budget psychological horror film would put him on the map for the first time. *The River's Edge* was dark, disturbing, and in many cases exploitive, but ultimately praised for its uncompromising daring. The movie focuses loosely on the real-life murder case in which a group of teens are forced into psychological and violent choices after a friend kills his girlfriend and disposes of the body. It was the kind of film where young actors leaped at the chance, but also had reservations. Keanu, of course, did not think twice about auditioning for the pivotal role of Matt.

Casting director Carrie Frazier, in a *Vice* interview, recalled the day Keanu walked into the room. "He walked in the door and I went 'Oh my god! Who is this guy?' It was the way he held his body. His shoes were untied and what he was wearing looked like a younger man changing into an older man. I was over the moon about him."

Reeves, whose character Matt plays a critical role in the film, acknowledged the disturbing and uncompromisingly horrifying elements to *The River's Edge*, but in conversation with *T&B*, recalled that the reason he took the part was a lot deeper than what was obvious. "It was about so much emotion. When I read the script, it wasn't robots I thought I was hearing. I heard pain and just so much emotion."

The movie *The Night Before* was light years removed from *The River's Edge* and was a gradual step for Keanu in the direction of blatant commercialism. It was a fairly mindless teen romp in which a teenager takes his girlfriend to the prom, loses consciousness and awakes in a dark alley only to discover that he has sold his prom date to a pimp. Keanu would have a good laugh in looking back on that film in the book *The New Breed: Actors Coming of Age*. "It seems that you have to do a kooky comedy to lose your Hollywood virginity, you know, guy wants girl, guy gets girl. It was a first for me in that I was in every scene."

The perception and maturity level of Keanu as something other than a teen boy-toy was upped in the film adaptation of *Dangerous Liaisons*, a pre-Revolutionary tale of sex, seduction and betrayal with a topnotch cast and location filming in France. Keanu, who was required to learn some French as well as a bit of swordplay for the part, recalled showing up for the audition in typical Keanu manner. He told *Playboy*, "When I auditioned, I'd been out biking and had on these holey pants and these big boots. I was coming on like Stanley Kowalski."

Keanu would hold his own, acting wise, during the production, alternately subtle in a natural way and expansive as needed. That *Dangerous Liaisons* was very much in the vein of Keanu's early attempts at theater indicated that the perception of the young, scruffy, often distracted-appearing actor was capable in what many considered an out-of-the box role.

Dangerous Liaisons would allow Keanu to travel the world for the first time as part of a major motion picture production. The production schedule was a bit off-kilter in that he was required to be in Paris for the shoot for a total of three months, while actually only shooting his scenes over a period of 15 days. Keanu took advantage of an abundance of off time as he explained to *Film Review*. "I spent most of my time drinking wine and cavorting around Paris."

Keanu would turn in another troubled teen role in *Permanent Record*, a suicide prevention-themed film in which Keanu's character, an aimless outsider with a close group of college friends, deal with the suicide of a close friend. By this time, Keanu had become dangerously close to being stereotyped as a teenage outsider. But the mature nature of the film did offer some signs that the adult in the portrayal was breaking through. Keanu was succinct about *Permanent Record*, in a warts and all conversation with *Choices*: "The movie is really about friendships and relationships but it's also very twisted."

Permanent Record would mark the end of a non-stop two-year run in which Keanu seemed to be working constantly, slowly but surely morphing into a more adult, assured performer. In looking back during an interview with *T&B.com*, Keanu seemed of two minds about his work to that point. "I've worked pretty hard for a couple of years. I think I've become kind of a freak, constantly playing younger than who I am. It affects me. I don't regret the roles but I want to catch up to myself."

CHAPTER EIGHT
KEANU: "I'M GOING TO DIE"

Sometimes Keanu will show people his scar.

Like every other facet of Keanu's psyche, lifting up his shirt and showing the long, mottled mass of scar tissue, running up and down his stomach, is a spur-of-the-moment thing, a spontaneous acknowledgement of a lifelong passion for big motorcycles and high speeds that has often left him bloodied but unbowed.

Keanu has acknowledged, with no small sense of pride, that said passion has turned him into a living mixture of scars, broken bones and shredded skin, all physical reminders that there can be drama and disaster connected to living for the open road

A passion for riding his motorcycle into the night is one that Keanu has often described to reporters in existential terms. "I love riding through Los Angeles on my own. With the wind, the sound," he offered to *The Daily Mail*. He also told *BB Magazine* that he was often the most invigorated when driving through the woods with others in the middle of the night. "With the lights off, with maybe two other people with me, and we'd tell each other what we saw. It was very cool."

At least it was during the spring of 1988. *The River's Edge* had been a critical and moderately commercial success. Keanu was now on everybody's radar and his reaction to the accolades, as well as a way to perhaps get away from it all, was to get on his bike and ride. He headed for Topanga Canyon Boulevard, a literal rollercoaster of hairpin turns and narrow winding roads that ended at the Pacific Ocean. Topanga Canyon Boulevard was legendary for causing bone-crushing accidents to overzealous riders and while it wasn't the road immortalized years earlier by the Jan and Dean song *"Deadman's Curve,"* it might as well have been, Reeves would, years later, reflect on that night in *Rolling Stone.* "I call that a demon ride. That's when things are going badly." Reeves further recalled that he was doing about 50 miles per hour when he hit a hairpin turn and ran into a hillside. He dramatically recalled the impact in *Rolling Stone.* "I remember saying in my head 'I'm going to die'."

Keanu lay sprawled on the pavement. He was having trouble breathing so he took off his helmet. Suddenly he heard the sound and saw the lights of an oncoming truck. Keanu managed to scramble out of the way just as the truck screamed around the corner and crushed his helmet. He spent the next half hour bruised, broken and hovering on the edge of life and death. "I remember calling out for help," he painfully recalled to *Rolling Stone.* "I remember someone answering out of the darkness and then there was the flashing lights of an ambulance coming toward me."

Keanu was rushed to a nearby hospital where doctors discovered that the accident had left him with a damaged spleen which was subsequently removed. Keanu would be much the worse for wear. And in typical Keanu manner, his tongue was firmly in his cheek when he offered to *Rolling Stone* just what that experience taught him. "I should have gone to the brake, released the brake a little bit and leaned into the turn. Now I know that if I want to take a 'demon ride' and I don't want to die... then I shouldn't take it."

CHAPTER NINE
KEANU'S WOMEN: PART I

Amanda De Cadenet was 19, pregnant and married to a rock star, Duran Duran bassist John Taylor, when she first laid eyes on Keanu on the UK TV talk show *The Word* in 1991. For Amanda, it was the classic case of love at first sight. Or it could have just as easily been lust.

"Within minutes of laying eyes on him, I remember thinking 'I wonder how many pregnant women have affairs'," Amanda said in her memoir *It's Messy: Essays on Boys, Boobs and Badass Women.* "I was surprised by strong attraction to Keanu, a man I had just met, said the model-actress, a notorious wild child well into the '90s.

Throwing caution to the wind, Amanda recalled making an all-too-obvious attempt to seduce him, recalling in her book that Keanu "spurned my advances. I discovered he was a man of hardcore ethics."

Some years later, Amanda and Taylor would divorce and, free, she once again set her sights on Keanu, with the pair occasionally getting together for dates. But to Amanda's undying disappointment, the dates would all be chaste. "From the day I got divorced, I tried every goddamned trick in the book to get him to submit to my advances. I even tried and tested seduction techniques that had worked for me 100 percent of the time. But they failed. Keanu was having none of it. And thank God because if we had become lovers, I don't think we would have had the powerful relationship we have today."

Paula Abdul. Lori Petty. If he worked with them or happened to pass them in a supermarket, the odds were good that Keanu and just about every woman in Hollywood would be linked in some segment of reality or speculation.

Yes, Keanu's love life, barely coming of age as a star in the late '80s and early '90s, was already the stuff of legend. Keanu's way of going through life, often solitary, cerebral and distracted, did not seem the stuff of women's dreams. However, once his career began to skyrocket, it turns out that Keanu was never at a loss of female companionship.

The press was constantly digging deep regarding Keanu's love life, with rumors and speculation running rampant, due, in large part, to the fact that Keanu was not a kiss and tell kind of guy and would deftly dodge and weave around any questions that got too personal. Occasionally, though, he would meet the subject head on, albeit philosophically.

"I want to get married," he told *Parade Magazine*. "I want to have kids. All that is at the top of the mountain and I've got to climb the mountain first." In a quote from *TheMind'sJournal.com*, Keanu made a compelling case for his isolation. "I'm single and I don't feel lonely. I take myself out to eat. I buy myself clothes. I have great times with myself. Once you know how to take care of yourself, company becomes an option and not a necessity."

This bit of true confession would do little to dissuade the perennial rumor that Keanu was truly involved and that his latest might well be "the one."

Keanu's next "romance" would turn out to be so quiet and low key that if you blinked you missed it. Just prior to Keanu going before the cameras in Francis Ford Coppola's film *Bram Stoker's Dracula*, the young actor made the acquaintance of Coppola's daughter, budding filmmaker Sofia. The pair clicked immediately and became a couple for the better part of a year before going their separate ways. They were not shy about their short-lived relationship, often being photographed walking together holding hands. To what degree it was serious or just a friendship has always been up for speculation. In an interview with *W Magazine*, Coppola described their relationship by saying "He's a friend." But it was noticed when scanning the credits of her directing debut, *Lost in Translation*, that Keanu was listed in the closing credits with a big thank you.

Keanu has never been known as a hardcore "hey baby" pickup artist but then came actress Sherrie Rose. According to a breathless *Star Magazine* report, Keanu and Rose ran into each other one night in 1992 at The Roxbury Club in Los Angeles. They had crossed paths in the acting world for two years and that was pretty much it. But on this night, sparks were definitely flying, as they embraced hotly on the dance floor before leaving, hand in hand, for Keanu's hotel room at the nearby Chateau Marmont. *The Star* offered alleged photographic evidence of the couple in a hot embrace before entering his hotel room, where they barely came up for air for two days. The consensus was that they were now officially lovers. But if they were, it was short lived.

The relationship between Keanu and actress Winona Ryder, which began, for all intents and purposes, in 1991-92 on the set of *Bram Stoker's Dracula,* is as contrary as it is insightful to Keanu's relationship mindset. The pair met when Winona was only 16 and, almost immediately, a relationship blossomed that was old-fashioned in nature. Winona assessed the early stages of their relationship in a conversation with *BlackBook.com.* "I've known Keanu since I was 16 and he's sort of been like a brother to me."

It was at Ryder's suggestion that Keanu be hired to play the pivotal role of Jonathan Harker in *Bram Stoker's Dracula.* During the filming Keanu and Winona's chaste relationship flourished as the like-minded souls bonded, helping to combat the often pressure-packed world of Hollywood. Winona was fond of keeping quite personal journals during that period and, in an excerpt published in *Vanity Fair*, Keanu was definitely on her mind. "Angst, angst, angst, angst. Thank God for Keanu. Thank God I'm going to see Keanu. I was always just so happy when you were around."

Post-*Dracula*, their friendship would continue in a number of films and in a very Spencer Tracy/Katherine Hepburn way. Of course, the press would regularly have a field day, speculating that the friends were actually lovers. Did they have those feelings? In a conversation with *Entertainment Tonight,* both conceded that early on there was a hint of that. "When we met in the '80s I had a huge crush on him," admitted Ryder. Keanu was quick to agree, offering, "I had a big, healthy crush on her too."

The close, yet platonic friendship has continued. The pair regularly exchange handwritten letters, an oddity in the techno age. Keanu has remained largely close-mouthed about his relationship with Winona. Winona is good naturedly more open and effusive when asked. "He's one of my favorite people to be around and to work around," she told *Entertainment Tonight.* "He always has my back," Winona told a *Today Show* interviewer. And she is quick to let people know how she really feels, telling *The Boston Globe* "Keanu knows I have a huge crush on him. I tell him all the time."

Ever the gentleman, Keanu summed up his feelings about Winona when he admitted, almost sheepishly, to *Entertainment Tonight,* "I feel the same about you."

Keanu's "feelings" would continue. It's safe to say that the young actor was seemingly never without female companionship, hardly living his life as a monk well into the '90s. But from the various gossip column and scandal rag reports, "chaste" and Keanu and Winona seemed to be going hand in hand.

Exhibit A? Sandra Bullock.

The pair met on the set of *Speed* and were immediately in "like." "I think about how sweet Keanu Reeves was and how handsome he was," Bullock gushed during an *Ellen DeGeneres Show* interview. "It was really hard for me to be serious [during the making of *Speed*]. He'd look at me and I'd just giggle."

When it came to Bullock, Keanu also was harboring less-than-professional feelings during the making of *Speed.* "She obviously didn't know that I had a crush on her too," he would tell *Ellen DeGeneres* during a separate talk show appearance. He acknowledged that he didn't want to reveal his secret crush to her because he wanted to remain professional. "We were working," was the reason stated for holding back his true feelings.

But despite any tension behind their mutual feelings, their relationship, again more brother/sister/ good friend than romantic, flourished during the making of *Speed*. "I had to read for *Speed* just to make sure the chemistry between Keanu and I was okay," Bullock told *Entertainment Weekly*. "We had to do all these physical scenes together and, at one point, Keanu stumbled into me and grabbed my butt. I asked him if he was trying to cop a feel? He got all panicky and was like 'No I wasn't!' I was like 'Relax, Keanu. I was just kidding.'"

She also regaled Ellen DeGeneres with an example of how gentlemanly Keanu could be, telling a story about *Speed's* action scenes. "During a lot of the scenes, my dress kept flying up and so, at one point, I asked Keanu if he could make sure my dress stayed down. He did and it was a very sweet thing for him to do."

Keanu would indirectly acknowledge that their secretly kept feelings for each other during the making of *Speed* was the main reason why their chemistry on screen was so believable. Later, in the name of keeping his personal life personal, walked back the question of his true feelings. "She's such a wonderful person," he told *Entertainment Weekly*. "I can't explain why Sandra and I have chemistry. We just do and I'm glad."

Bullock would, years later, take a stab about why the relationship between her and Keanu worked. In a conversation with *CinemaBlend.com*, she explained, "There's a sense of ease for me working with Keanu. It's an ease for me to look at him in situations where I'm just not comfortable with myself. I can look him in the eye and feel that I have a place there."

After *Speed*, Bullock and Keanu went on to become literal best friends and non-existent as lovers.

There appeared to be a pattern developing that, while he is always looking for love, there is also a real respect for women that is just as important as a romantic relationship. That quality plays out in various ways.

It has long been Keanu's policy to stand behind women when posing for pictures and not physically touch them. With Bullock, it has been an exception, as countless photos of the pair show Keanu's arm around Bullock's waist or holding her hand. Another modification brought on by his relationship with Bullock centers on his longstanding reluctance to appear at charity or other public events. It is a policy that has mellowed during his relationship with Bullock, with the actor regularly appearing at events where Bullock was also present. They keep in constant contact by text, as well as via that now-archaic form of communication called the handwritten letter. They have occasionally been spotted having dinner dates, or seen in each other's company at a function, which continues to fuel the speculation that Bullock and Keanu are more than just friends.

That speculation that was put to Bullock on *Entertainment Tonight,* when the actress was asked if she had ever tried to set up the perpetually single Keanu with somebody. Bullock laughed at that notion. "He doesn't need anybody's help setting him up. He's good."

CHAPTER TEN
KEANU'S EXCELLENT ADVENTURE

Keanu went into the late '80s maddeningly contrary on any number of personal and professional fronts. He had just turned 24 but, in looks and demeanor, he could still pass for 18. He continued to parlay a biting sense of humor and the ability to be spontaneously quotable, to his best advantage, especially when it came to questions of a professional nature. He'd often have interviewers dancing around trying to figure out what was sincere and what was simply Keanu pulling the media's collective leg.

Sometimes Keanu would say something, then crack a devilish smile to let the interviewer know that it was a joke, or at the very least, an exaggeration. There were the times when an answer would be preceded by endless moments of silence as Keanu contemplated the impact of what he was about to say. And then there were those times when Keanu would give a long verbal dance that ended up with the question not being answered. But most of the time, Keanu seemed willing to play along. Prime examples being…

"I'm 24," he offered *Film Review*. "I can't play kids all my life." But he was just as quick to flip the switch and play the ultimate mercenary when he talked to

Young Americans Magazine. "Soaps, sitcoms, dramas, I don't care. What would I do for a million bucks? Absolutely anything. I'm shameless." Turn the figurative page and reporters would see yet another side, as in a *Newsday* interview when the enigmatic actor offered. "I just want to do amazing work with amazing people and, hopefully, before I die, I won't be too sad and pathetic." Keanu, with tongue firmly planted in cheek, suggested to the *Los Angeles Times* that "As people get to know me better, I'll start to get the sleazier roles."

While he had gotten to the point where he was getting the kind of offers that most actors on the rise would kill for, Keanu was, in fact, saying no to things as well both for aesthetic and philosophical reasons. When Oliver Stone offered him the starring role in *Platoon* (which ultimately went to Charlie Sheen), his aversion to what he perceived as the extreme violence in the film drove him to say "thanks, but no thanks." Stone summed up Keanu's rejection this way. "Keanu turned it down because of the violence," he told *Entertainment Weekly*. "H didn't want to do violence." Keanu would have a much more simple reason for turning down the lead in the much anticipated sequel *The Fly II*. "I didn't like the script," he told *Entertainment Weekly*.

Perhaps most telling were those moments when he was being serious, ironic and raw in the same breath, as when told *Another Man* magazine "I guess I'm just doing what I'm doing, trying at least. Trying to survive and hopefully not get fucked up the ass by irony and the gods."

The offer to co-star in *Bill & Ted's Excellent Adventure* was anything but sleazy but, to many observers, the project seemed a bit suspect. On the surface, *Bill & Ted's Excellent Adventure*, in which the titular high school slackers travel through time to assemble historical figures for their high school history presentation, was a blatant, exploitive, obvious and let's be honest, on the high side of moronic science fiction comedy. One that, despite its inherent dumbness, seemed to have some potential in the teenage market and a bit of questionable cachet. Consequently, the line to audition was considerable, with the likes of Pauly Shore, River Phoenix, Sean Penn and Brendan Fraser vying for the role of Bill. As it turned out, Keanu was the first actor to audition for the role of Ted, and the producers were so impressed that they immediately gave him the part.

Although Keanu was initially leery about playing yet another adolescent of limited intellect, as the production progressed he admitted to *Starlog* magazine that he was finding much in the character to latch onto. "I'm having the best time. I'm playing a guy who's so insouciant, such a naïve child of the woods, that it's been fun and cleansing."

But contrary to the image he was presenting to the public, Keanu was a no-bullshit kind of guy when assessing the relative worth of his films, and *Bill & Ted's Excellent Adventure* was no exception. He spoke to *Movieline,* saying, "It's not like I'm Robert De Niro in *Raging Bull* in this film. But if *Bill & Ted* is going to be my claim to fame… well then that's going to be my claim to fame."

Initially there had been talk of releasing *Bill & Ted's Excellent Adventure* direct to video, but a more daring studio would prevail and the film would be released to theaters in February 1989. Bottom line, the target audience of teens got it and turned the modestly budgeted movie into a $40 million mega-hit. The success of the film did, by association, begin to draw attention to Keanu. And the consensus was that while Keanu remained a bit rough around the edges, his talent as an actor could not be denied.

The result was that 1990-91 was a period of growth as Keanu began to work with big-time directors and actors in blockbuster commercial hit *Parenthood* and the critically applauded lesser films *I Love You to Death* and *Tune In Tomorrow*. The unexpected success of *Bill & Ted's Excellent Adventure* quickly brought about talks of a sequel. Even though Keanu seemed to be rapidly growing his resume with more mature roles in bigger films, the realist and, perhaps a little bit of mercenary in him, quickly had him agreeing to bring back Ted in the sequel.

"Work is work," Keanu told *Film Review*. "I've sort of accepted that I'm still going to be offered teen parts for a while so I might as well make the most of them."

CHAPTER ELEVEN
KEANU'S JUST THE BASS PLAYER

Keanu was a big Joy Division fan from way back and a follower of most modern music in general. But he readily admitted that he had no desire to be a rock star, let alone even consider playing an instrument. All that changed in 1990 when Keanu had an epiphany. "I just remember one day I was walking down the street in Los Angeles and, I don't know, I suddenly had a desire to play it (bass)," he related in *Paloaltoonline.com*. "I guess it's just from liking the sound of it. My ear was drawn to it in the music I listen to. And I wanted to play an instrument."

Keanu bought a bass and, after one lesson with somebody whose name had long slipped his mind, was completely self-taught. The connection between Keanu and the bass grew as he slowly but surely mastered the complexities of the instrument to a level of competency. "I loved the sound of the instrument," Keanu offered in a *Jakarta Post* interview. "I loved the physicality of playing it."

Keanu would remain a closeted musician until 1991, when, while cruising the aisle of a Los Angeles supermarket, he ran into actor/musician Robert Millhouse, sporting a Detroit Red Wings hockey jersey.

Keanu sensed a kindred spirit and asked Robert if he was looking for a goalie. Keanu chronicled the odyssey in *ETC* magazine. "We used to get together because we both loved hockey, so it wasn't about music at first. I wasn't even thinking about being in a band. But I had some space in my house and one day Robert suggested that we have a jam. At first it was just a case of us making a lot of noise." It was about that time that things got a bit more serious, with the inclusion of Gregg Miller. And just like that, Keanu's place in rock music lore began.

Keanu picked up the story in an interview with television talk show host Jimmy Fallon. "We started in a garage. Then we ended up starting to write songs. Then we were like 'let's go out and play them.'" Before they could get real gigs, the band needed a name. In short order, they called themselves Small Fecal Matter and Big Fucking Shit before deciding on a more literate name, Dogstar, a name mentioned in the Henry Miller novel *Sexus.*

Dogstar's very first gig was in a Los Angeles dive bar called Raji's in front of approximately 60 people. Dogstar was the headliner, but the gig was also significant for the fact that the opening act was another unknown band that would soon become very big, Weezer. They would also headline an early show at The Troubadour. Ever so slowly, Dogstar began its march through the Los Angeles club scene.

From the outset, Keanu did his best to be nothing more than a member of the band. During performances, he would hang in the background, rarely looking up and conceding the prerequisite rock star moments to the rest of the band. But ultimately, it would be a losing battle.

Keanu was coming of age as a major motion picture star and, while Dogstar was a decent band in those days, with an enticing mixture of grunge, punk and mainstream sensibilities that often saw them mixing band originals with covers of such disparate bands as Joy Division, The Jam, Neil Young and Fugazi, Dogstar as a band quickly fell victim to having Keanu as a member.

Dogstar would often be referred to as "Keanu's band" and reviewers and interviewers would almost completely focus their attention on Keanu who, to his credit, would often defer to the other band members in interview situations. But more often than not, it would be a losing battle. To their credit, the rest of Dogstar were mature enough and realistic enough to deal with the attention being primarily on their bass player.

Dogstar member Bret Domrose summed up the highs and lows of having Keanu in the band in conversation with *ETC*. "Having Keanu in the band is a double-edged sword. A lot of good comes from it and a lot of bad. This is a band and when people single him out all the time, that angers me a lot. But it's not Keanu's fault."

Keanu was ever the diplomat in the same *ETC* piece when he offered, "I'm grateful for the publicity my movie career gives the band. I realize the audiences are coming to see the band because of it but if it brings them to see us I'm happy because at least it gives the band a chance to be heard."

Into the mid '90s, Dogstar began to progress. There would be memorable gigs with the likes of David Bowie and Bon Jovi, a mammoth two-month tour of Europe and Asia, a short-lived record deal with Zoo Entertainment and the growing idea that the band

61

was becoming less of a Keanu vanity project and more of a viable musical entity. The band would release two albums, *Our Little Visionary* in 1996 (also known as *Quattro Formaggi,* released under the *Our Little Visionary* title after the deal with Zoo Entertainment fell apart prior to the release of *Quattro Formaggi*) and *Happy Ending* in the year 2000.

But the reality remained that with Keanu, the steady climb was stop and start. When Keanu spent seven months shooting the film *Devil's Advocate* opposite Al Pacino, Dogstar ground to a halt. Keanu had entered the stage of his career where he was constantly in demand for film projects he could not say no to. But the remaining members of Dogstar were quick to point out than when he was finished with a film, he would quickly come back to the band. Keanu was seen as somebody who was serious about having both an acting and a music career.

"I'm just as committed to the band as I am to acting," he insisted to *ETC*. "Hopefully I will be able to do both."

Dogstar would carry on in fits and starts until 2002, when Keanu's increased film schedule, combined with the remainder of the band's desire to tour and to do the work to become full-blown rock stars, brought the band to an end. For the record, Dogstar's last appearance would be a sold-out concert in Osaka, Japan on October 12, 2002. And all reports indicated that a good time was had by all.

CHAPTER TWELVE
KEANU AND RIVER... OVER AND OUT

The first time River Phoenix set eyes on Keanu, he watched as his ex-girlfriend and the actor were making out.

"Actually, I met Keanu through my ex-girlfriend Martha Plimpton while they were doing *Parenthood* (which also featured River's brother Joaquin)," recalled Phoenix in a quote from an extensive file called *MyRiverPhoenixCollection.com* by way of *Interview.* "They were sucking face regularly during the making of that film. At that point I wasn't even a friend of his."

But that changed when the pair appeared in the dark comedy *I Love You to Death*. It was evident that Keanu and River came from the same place. They were young stars on the rise in Hollywood, and both had come from relatively unorthodox family backgrounds, and shared a spiritual/naturalistic ethic that had them shying away from the glitz and glamour of Tinseltown. But the fact that they bonded on an immediate level of "best friend" went a lot deeper than that.

At the time, Keanu was effusive about the depth of his feeling for River. "River is a real good friend," he said in a quote from *MyRiverPhoenixCollection.com*. "He's so uncomplicated. He's beautiful, inventive, funny and creative. He asks questions that I don't normally think about. He works in a way that, at least for me, showed me how to get it more in my blood and my imagination." River, in the *MyRiverPhoenixCollection.com*, also talked about his relationship with Keanu as something special. "Keanu is someone you can tell all your secrets to. He's a guy you enjoy being with, a guy you love and a guy you care about. Keanu is my buddy."

It was during the production of *I Love You To Death* that the personal and professional nature of their relationship was tested when their respective agents received the script for *My Own Private Idaho* from director Gus Van Zant, who, from the outset, only had eyes for Keanu and River to play the two male prostitutes on a downward physical and emotional slide.

Keanu was interested, based largely on the fact that *My Own Private Idaho*, which in a broad sense, resonated with the vibe of *Henry IV, Part 1*, *Henry IV, Part 2* and *Henry V,* which appealed to the Shakespeare in the young actor. Reeves would reveal his initial hesitancy years later in an interview with *Interview* when he recalled, "I was overwhelmed at what I had to do. It was like 'Oh no! Can I do this? I was afraid.' "

Getting River to go along with it was a whole other matter. *Paper Magazine* reported that River's agent was so aghast that she stopped reading halfway down the first page of the script and refused to let her client see it, let alone consider doing it. But director Van Zant was dead-set on Keanu and River doing the film, and went around River's agent to Keanu and suggested that it would be in everybody's best interest if he hand carried the script to River personally.

Keanu agreed and, in December 1990, while in

Toronto, he jumped on his 1974 Norton Commando motorcycle and, with script in hand, drove 1,300 miles to the Phoenix family compound in Gainesville, Florida, and handed the script to River. River liked the film but his bond with Keanu at the time was strong, so it ultimately boiled down to a final pact that was made sometime later when, in Los Angeles, the pair were riding together down Santa Monica Boulevard when, in true blood brother fashion, the deal was sealed.

Keanu remembered that moment well in conversation with *Interview*. "We were driving in a car on Santa Monica Blvd, probably on our way to a club and talking really fast about the whole idea. We were excited. It could have been a bad dream, a dream that never follows through because no one ever commits. But we forced ourselves into it. Finally, we said 'Okay. I'll do it if you do it. I won't do it if you won't. We shook hands. That was it."

There was a sense of simplicity and finality in that handshake. For the two close friends it was as simple as that.

The chemistry as friends effectively translated into their powerful, often gut-wrenching performances in *My Own Private Idaho*, a movie that would be awarded critical raves, with reviews touting both Keanu and River's performances as their best to date.

But there was a sense that River was slowly spiraling down during the making of the film. Reports filtering out of the set were that River was drinking a lot and using drugs on occasion, a combination that would escalate into full-blown addiction after the completion of the film. Not surprisingly, Keanu remained ever supportive of River, years later talking guardedly about his friend, in interview excerpts that appeared in *MyRiverPhoenixCollection.com.*

"River had a self-destructive side to his personality. He was angry and hurt that he couldn't have a private life once he became famous. He just couldn't deal with having his private life on the front page all the time. River felt differently about things than I do. He allowed the suffering of the world to get to him and he wanted everyone to be as free and happy as he was. I live a real low key life and I like to deal with pressures in other ways."

Other projects saw Keanu and River go their separate ways following the completion of *My Own Private Idaho.* Keanu went the action route with *Point Blank* and the movie that would ultimately break him as a top draw international star, *Speed.* Keanu was in the middle of shooting *Speed* when he received the news. River had died of a drug overdose in front of the notorious rock club The Viper Room on October 31, 1993.

Keanu went into an emotional shell at the news. He was on the verge of mega-stardom, but none of that seemed to ring true. Because Keanu, in the midst of his greatest professional triumph, was in a very dark place.

The *Speed* production had quickly become a family. They immediately saw Keanu's pain and did what they could to ease it. *Speed* director Jan De Bont told *Entertainment Weekly* that he immediately rearranged the action-packed filming schedule for a few days to give Keanu easier scenes to do. "The death of River got to Keanu emotionally," De Bont remembered. "He became very quiet and it took him quite a while to work it out by himself and to calm down. It (River's death) had scared the hell out of him."

In the ensuing days, Keanu went about his business, performing both the action sequences and romantic scenes with a workmanlike sense of purpose. He was a professional, and those who have seen *Speed* would be hard-pressed to know the strain he was under. But the cast and crew were fully aware.

The production continued under a cloud of sadness and silence. Nobody talked about River's death, especially to Keanu. But there was a sense of the loss that the young actor was feeling. Years later, Keanu's co-star, Sandra Bullock, would reflect on what Keanu must have been going through during the subsequent days on the *Speed*, telling *Tele 7 Jours* magazine, "I think that he has gone through a lot even though he does not let on about it. I think he hides a great pain."

For a time, the first major personal trauma of the death of his best friend would seemingly be handled in stages for Keanu. In a *Rolling Stone* article, a close friend who asked to remain anonymous would disclose that, early on, nobody in his close inner circle would talk to Keanu about River. But that would not stop the prying eyes of the media from broaching the question of River to Keanu. Initially his response would be either no comment or a sullen look that was shorthand for not wanting to talk about it. As time went on, he would seemingly become resigned to the fact that he could not escape speaking about it. That's when he began opening up about his feelings.

"I miss him," Keanu simply said at one point in an interview with *Entertainment Weekly*. "I miss him greatly." When he was finally capable of addressing his friend's death, Keanu acknowledged in a *Parade* interview that, "I enjoyed his company. I enjoyed his mind. I enjoyed his spirit and his soul."

Although the grief over River's death has never really left him, Keanu, by degrees, had at least become able to deal with it. He became more spiritual and philosophical in contemplating the first great personal loss in his life. But the raw humanity of the tragedy would never really leave him, the bottom line, as he offered to *Tele 7 Jours* was simply…

… "What can I say? I miss him a lot."

CHAPTER THIRTEEN
A SHORT COURSE IN KEANU
GETTING HIGH

Keanu did such a good job playing stoner Ted in *Bill & Ted's Excellent Adventure* that many critics were convinced that he may well have been high during the making of the film. Cooler heads jumped to Keanu's defense, proclaiming that his portrayal was simply the result of being a very good actor.

In real life, Keanu often presented an image to the world that, yes, he was indeed high. Bottom line, Keanu has taken drugs. But, as he offered in a *Rolling Stone* interview, "It hasn't been in a blue moon. But I do once in a while."

There is much in evidence that Keanu was taking drugs post *Bill & Ted* in the early '90s, a lot of pot and a lot of what he calls hallucinogenic drugs. And to this day, he remains a staunch advocate of drug use as a psychological and creative tool.

"I've had wonderful experiences with drugs," he told *Vanity Fair*. "I mean really wonderful." He furthered his pro-drug stance in conversation with *Rolling Stone* when he said, "Drugs certainly helped me to see more or having the sensation of seeing more. I guess part of the hallucinogenic… the feelings one has. The seeing, feeling and looking at nature and seeing what comes out of one's self and having parts of the psyche revealed. Drugs have certainly given me a level of enrichment."

But Keanu's drug ride has not always been positive. To this day, stories, rumors and half-truths continue to surface from his days on the set of *My Own Private Idaho*. The more "out there: reports indicated that director Gus Van Zant allegedly encouraged drug use by Keanu and River Phoenix in order to get believable performances out of them. The story that River was in the throes of full-blown drug addiction, involving heroin, continue to be part of film lore. While those reports stop short of Keanu doing anything more than "partying hard" during the making of that film, the consensus was that Keanu, while not addicted, may well have been a willing participant in drug use at the time.

Another incident in Keanu's drug life may have been on display during the making of *Bill & Ted's Excellent Adventure*, when the actor was found slumped over in his trailer and was rushed to the hospital. The incident was blamed on a reaction to an arm infection. But more than one scandal sheet, and in particular *The Star*, speculated that Keanu's collapse may have had more to do with the ingestion of a "mystery substance."

Throughout his life, Keanu continued to be upfront in his drug use and, during 1991-92, he freely admitted to *Vanity Fair* that his reputation as an actor who took drugs was making the rounds of Hollywood. "I had a reputation in Hollywood of being a drug user. And because of that, I did some things professionally that I wouldn't have normally done if I didn't have to.

I did a Japanese commercial in order to be able to pay my rent. I did a Paula Abdul music video because I needed the money."

But with age, moderation has become Keanu's watch word when it comes to certain substances. And he is quick to point out as much when he told *Rolling Stone*…

…"I never had a bad trip."

CHAPTER FOURTEEN
THE EXISTENTIAL ACTION HERO

Going into the early '90s, it appeared that professionally, Keanu was coming of age. With the success of the two *Bill & Ted* films and the good notices from *My Own Private Idaho*, the young actor was starting to appear bankable in a number of genres and on a number of fronts. Comparisons, admittedly often more hype than reality, were being favorably made to Marlon Brando and Steve McQueen. But at a time when Keanu should have been over the moon, he was still philosophically adrift.

His perceived status in the industry, Keanu was quick to tell the *Toronto Sun,* was that he still felt unsure of where he stood. "It's not the scariest part of my life but then it is a lot of mystery because I don't know what my next acting job is. I'm 26 and something happened when I went from 25 to 26. I started asking myself 'What am I doing here and what's going on?'"

What was going on was simply Keanu being Keanu, a far cry from the perception of a Hollywood movie star as somebody, figuratively and literally, always on the hunt. He remained largely a loner who, by his own admission, rarely was out and about in Hollywood. While he would do interviews, he did so grudgingly and was often seemingly nervous, halting and inarticulate when dealing with the media. And nobody knew his shortcomings better than Keanu himself, who admitted as much in conversation with *BB Magazine*. "I don't know what to say. I can tell you that I had fun doing this or that but I just can't organize my thoughts."

One of his more lucid responses during this period would center on the fear of stereotyping, which surfaced during a largely softball interview with *Just 17*. Long story short, Keanu had been so good as the gay male hustler in *My Own Private Idaho* that there was an undercurrent of fear in and out of the industry that he might be pigeonholed by the Hollywood when it came to certain roles. "I don't think it will hurt my career because I'm not trying to be a star, I'm trying to be an actor. You have to put the love of your craft before fame and money. Fame can ruin you in a lot of ways. It can influence you to make bad decisions."

Bottom line, he could definitely act, but when it came to those Hollywood intangibles that defined stardom, Keanu was still, in many cases, missing the mark. Which, as he offered in an interview with *Dolly Magazine*, was by design. "I don't want to become a Hollywood product machine. I'm not really interested in being the main guy on the screen. I love playing small parts. All I need to do is support myself."

But despite Keanu's best efforts, the "Hollywood machine" would come looking for him in the guise of a very mainstream action film called *Point Break*. *Point Break*, a high-octane action/adventure film in which an FBI agent infiltrates a gang of daring surfer bank robbers called the Ex Presidents, had been kicking around Hollywood since 1986, with no less a director than Ridley Scott attached. A list of marquee-name actors, including Val Kilmer, Charlie Sheen, Johnny Depp and Mathew Broderick were being considered for the role of FBI agent Johnny Utah. But when director Kathryn Bigelow took over the film's reins, she saw something in Keanu's demeanor and the way he handled himself on camera that made him the ideal choice to play a buttoned-down law man who goes deep underground in an alien culture to get the bad guys.

Keanu saw *Point Break* as being good fun and liked the notion of Bigelow bringing new progressive ideas to the tried-and-true action tropes and was excited about working with fellow cast members Patrick Swayze, Gary Busey and Lori Petty. From a career point of view it also made sense. It was a big; a slam-bang action movie from a major studio that would be seen on a lot of screens and make a lot of money— exactly the thing an actor flirting with stardom wanted on his resume. The physical aspect of making *Point Break…* well, that was a whole other story.

"I really got worked," Keanu quipped to the *Toronto Sun.* Bigelow was big on realism and wanted her actors to be as authentic as possible in every scene. So much so that Keanu trained for months prior to the start of filming to, in no particular order, learn how to play a believable FBI agent, a football quarterback, learn to surf and how to take and throw a punch. "The only thing I didn't learn to do was skydiving free fall," Keanu told the *Toronto Sun*, noting the limitations the production company put on the actors for insurance purposes. But ever a stickler for method acting to project the proper image on-screen, Keanu, unbeknownst to the filmmakers, took it upon himself to take four hours of skydiving training and then make one actual jump of 12,500 feet.

Point Break was conspicuous by its constant adrenaline rush, an over-the-top, yet effective depiction of masculinity and male bonding and the ease in which Bigelow ran roughshod over the cast and crew. Keanu was duly impressed. "Kathryn pushed everyone on the picture," he explained to *MovieLab.com*. "She wanted the audience right there. She wanted people surfing, driving, flipping and running. She pushed us all the time. With Kathryn, it was always 'Let's go!'"

Point Break would go on to become a massive international hit right out of the box and was instantly relegated to the realm of hip cult favorite. The film, in the best possible way, has followed Keanu to this day. People always stop him on the street and regale him with stories of how the film changed their lives. Keanu had to admit that *Point Break* had changed his life as well.

While on the surface, it appeared that Keanu was on a non-stop odyssey of all work and no play, the actor, in a 1993 *Detour* interview, did acknowledge that he did, in fact, get time off, and that those moments can often be as emotionally demanding as when he's working. "There's always a transition. I've finished a project and, all of a sudden, I come out the other side, look around me and I'm a little bewildered and in wonder of it all. The second day after I finish work, I'm full of angst and the classic feeling that I'm never going to work again. That usually lasts about a month, and after that I sit down again and enjoy the days."

The offers would continue to come in. At one point, Keanu was in the sights of director Oliver Stone for the role of rocker Jim Morrison for his movie *The Doors*. Keanu thought the role would be interesting and endured several auditions before watching as the role went to Val Kilmer. "I auditioned a few times," Keanu was quoted in *Collider.com*. "But I didn't think I was seriously in the running. I just read some of Jim Morrison's poetry, listened to some of his music and just did what I could."

As befitting the star of a breakout action hit, Keanu was bombarded with variations of the same post *Point Break*; big action films with him as the stalwart hero. But true to his mercurial nature, Keanu had other ideas. Although he loved the audition process, Keanu's profile had risen to the point where he would now primarily audition with a director. And through 1992-93, he would choose to primarily shy away from big flashy studio productions in favor of secondary roles in films of a more intimate nature with directors of merit. The one exception during this period would be the big studio production *Bram Stoker's Dracula,* directed by Francis Ford Coppola.

Keanu acknowledged in *Detour* that he learned a lot from Coppola on a subliminal level. "From Coppola, I got to witness a creative, industrious idea. He's a man of many ideas. He creates things."

More of a good-natured trifle, Keanu's appearance in the Kenneth Branagh adaptation of the Shakespearian romp *Much Ado About Nothing* indicated that Keanu's talents were travelling well in the filmmaking hierarchy, as offered by Branagh in *Detour*. "I've seen a sense of truthfulness in Keanu's work. When I met him he was someone I admired and liked his sort of curiosity and enthusiasm." Keanu also worked with famed director

Bernardo Bertolucci in the lavish period drama *Little Buddha*.

The chance to once again work with director Gus Van Zant resulted in Keanu doing what was ostensibly a cameo in the adaptation of the Tom Robbins novel *Even Cowgirls Get the Blues*. The opportunity to participate with the directorial debut of *Bill & Ted* co-star Alex Winter's indie, low-budget science fiction comedy *Freaked* resulted in the actor doing an uncredited cameo as Ortiz The Dog Boy.

None of these films were breakout hits and, in all candor, *Even Cowgirls Get the Blues* was a commercial bomb. But these lesser-known efforts on Keanu's resume fueled the notion that Keanu was an actor who was not afraid to detour from the expected and to take creative and career chances. Given his post *Point Break* leanings, Keanu made a surprise turn when he was approached with the script for *Speed,* in which a Los Angeles police officer on the trail of a mad bomber finds himself aboard a busload of passengers rigged with a bomb set to explode if the bus drops below 50 miles per hour.

Although the likes of Stephen Baldwin, Tom Cruise, Tom Hanks, Wesley Snipes and Woody Harrelson were reported to be sniffing around the title role of hero cop Jack Traven, *Speed* director Jan De Bont needed only to see *Point Break* to realize that Keanu was his guy, as he offered in an *Entertainment Weekly* feature. "What is nice about Keanu is that he comes across as vulnerable on the screen. He's not threatening to men because he's not that bulky and he looks great to women."

In Hollywood shorthand, *Speed* was *Die Hard* on a

bus. Reading between the lines of that initial draft of the script, Keanu was of two different minds. "I remember the script and it was like Eh?" he recalled in *Esquire*. "The plot was ridiculous." But after he stopped holding his nose in a critical sense, Keanu saw something deeper than typical slam bang and explosions. "The movie was attempting to bring an element of realism to action films," he related in a *Los Angeles Times* interview. "It plays on very real anxieties, the fear of elevators, buses and public places."

But while he liked the concept and deeper message, Keanu felt that the initial draft of the script was, pardon the pun, not up to speed. "The character was very flippant," he told *Entertainment Weekly*. "There were situations set up for one liners and I felt it was forced, kind of like *Die Hard* mixed with some kind of screwball comedy. I wasn't really interested in that. I thought we could do better."

De Bont agreed and a rewrite of the script, and with an emphasis on being straightforward and earnest rather than jokey, gave Keanu exactly what he wanted. But there would be a tradeoff involved in Keanu getting what he wanted.

De Bont wanted a cleaner-looking Jack Traven, somebody less hippie and more grown-up was the way he described it. Which meant that Keanu would have to physically transform his everyday look into something more mature and adult. Keanu had no problem with the notion that his long hair would be the first casualty of *Speed* and, in typical Keanu manner, the actor went to the opposite extreme by shaving his head completely. De Bont had a good laugh at the moment the freshly shaved actor walked into the director's office, telling

Entertainment Weekly, "Everyone at the studio was scared shitless when they first saw him. There was only like a millimeter of hair left."

While Keanu's hair would eventually grow back to a film-friendly length, the actor was also in the middle of a two-month workout program designed to give him upper body and arm musculature. Keanu did not want a Sly (Stallone) or Arnold (Schwarzenegger) physique, but he did manage to pack on 30 additional pounds. To say the least, Keanu did a double take the first time he looked at the finished product in the mirror. "I looked totally different," he offered *Just 17 Magazine.* "I didn't have a neck anymore. My head was just resting on my body with nothing in between. My face looked rounder which made my eyes look smaller."

Despite his experience in *Point Break*, Keanu was initially leery of the level of dangerous stunts that predominated in *Speed.* But through the subtle coaxing of director De Bont, he eventually got his nerve back and was more than willing to do much of the action, to the point where, unbeknownst to De Bont, Keanu was secretly learning the particulars of a scene in which his character jumps from a moving bus to a car. De Bont, on the day of that particular scene being shot, realized he had created a monster when Keanu insisted he do the stunt and held his breath until the scene was shot and his actor emerged unscathed.

The death of his good friend River Phoenix most certainly added some internal emotion and depth to Keanu's role as an everyman superhero, an element of the film that made numerous human moments stand out within the craziness and carnage. Keanu would emerge from *Speed* a more well-defined actor capable of playing just about anything that came his way. In typical Hollywood fashion, the early pre-release screenings of the film were extremely positive and, in the hallways of Hollywood were heard dollars-and-cents speculation that Keanu would be the next big-time action hero.

Keanu would take it all with a grain of salt. "I don't have any ambition to do that," he told *Entertainment Weekly*. "I'm not averse to working in the action genre again. It was good clean fun. But my ambition is variety."

And, unbeknownst to his cast and crewmates, during the making of *Speed*, he had already set his mind on the next big adventure. He was learning the lines to *Hamlet*. "I would finish playing Jack and would go into my trailer and it would be like 'How all occasions inform against me/And spur my own revenge/.' There was definitely a yin and yang thing going on."

At a time when Keanu was on the verge of his biggest commercial hit, a well-thumbed copy of *Hamlet* was taking him to another place "I'd grown up with Shakespeare," he told *Esquire*. "I had the training and the experience."

CHAPTER FIFTEEN
KEANU LANDS IN MOVIE JAIL

Speed hit theaters like a bomb. The best kind of bomb. On a fairly miniscule budget (by Hollywood action standards) of $38 million, *Speed* would go on to gross more than $350 million. But by the time Keanu's star was blazing across Hollywood like... well a runaway bus, Keanu was suffering a bad case of action movie fatigue.

Shortly after completing *Speed*, Keanu signed on opposite Morgan Freeman in an action-heavy thriller called *Chain Reaction,* with Keanu playing a scientist who invents a new power source and soon finds himself on the run from the FBI. A quote from Keanu in *Looper.com* indicated that Keanu was not thrilled with the results. "The process of making the movie was unsatisfying. I had to do a lot of running and action and it was disappointing."

But the executives at the studio did not really care. All they knew was that *Speed* had made a lot of money and that they wanted a *Speed 2*. And they were certain that if they could get the original cast and director back that it would make bank. This example of Hollywood-think was rewarded when De Bont was eager to return. and came up with what he felt was an ideal follow-up in which our happily-ever-after couple from the original *Speed* are on a cruise ship when they run afoul of yet another mad bomber.

Bullock was not thrilled with the idea of what would be called *Speed 2: Cruise Control*, but would make a calculating business deal with 20th Century Fox: She would do *Speed 2* in exchange for the studio funding the production of a much more modest pet project called *Hope Floats*. The only missing piece to this sequel puzzle was Keanu, and both De Bont and Bullock took it upon themselves to travel to Chicago in an attempt to convince the actor to return for *Speed 2*. By this time, Keanu had read an early draft of the script and, as he explained in subsequent interviews with both *The Telegraph* and *The Toronto Sun*, he was having none of it.

"Sandra and Jan were saying, 'You've got to do this!' And I said, 'I read the script and I can't. It's called *Speed* and it's on a boat. I just wasn't mentally and physically ready to do that picture. I could afford to say no because I had money and could pay my rent."

But 20th Century Fox was not about to give up without a fight. On his next trip to Los Angeles, Keanu met with then 20th Century Fox Film Entertainment head William Mechanic, who figuratively waved a check for $12 million in Keanu's face to get him to agree to *Speed 2*. Keanu was quietly offended at what he perceived as a not-too-subtle bribe and recalled as much in conversation with *The Telegraph*. "I told him (Mechanic) that if I do this film, I will not come back up. You guys will send me to the bottom of the ocean and I will not make it back up again. I really felt like I was fighting for my life."

The studio did not take Keanu's rejection well. And it resulted in 20th Century Fox stating for the record that Keanu had turned down *Speed 2* in order to go on tour with his band Dogstar. Keanu would go public in denying Fox's stories as nothing more than rumors generated by the studio, who he would subtly accuse the studio of being a sore loser. The resultant hard feelings ended up with 20th Century Fox putting Keanu in what the press described as "movie jail" essentially blackballing Keanu from any of their studio films for the next 14 years.

Not content to merely rub one studio the wrong way, Keanu turned right around and said no to a pivotal role in the Warner Bros. crime drama *Heat* that toplined two of his idols, Robert DeNiro and Al Pacino. The reason he turned down *Heat* was a bit more cut and dried. Quite simply, Keanu had received a better offer.

Live theater.

The Manitoba Theater Center in Winnipeg, Canada had a long and sterling reputation for putting on superior productions of the classics and drawing big-name actors who wished to showcase their talents in a more intimate place than the big screen could offer. For his part, Keanu was entertaining the thought of performing strictly as an experiment that only he could imagine. Keanu had something to prove, so, as the fallout from turning his back on two major motion pictures rained down on him from his management, agents and the studios, Keanu began to lay plans to exercise an opportunity to fail.

It was a stealth operation, with Keanu swearing his agent and management to secrecy. And a first step was to reconnect with his Canadian theater roots. Manitoba Theater Center artistic director Steven Schipper went back a long way with Keanu. When Keanu was only 16, Schipper auditioned him for a small part in a Sam Shepard play. As it turned out, Keanu was too tall for the role, but Schipper remained impressed by the young actor's talent. Consequently he was intrigued when Keanu contacted him about the possibility of acting in a theater production.

He knew the publicity value of Keanu acting in a Manitoba Theater Center production would be significant. He also realized that it could be a total fiasco if Keanu's chops were not up to the task. But, as he explained to *Macleans,* "Keanu's had a very successful film career because that's what he's pursued. But I have no doubt, had he pursued a career on stage, he would have established an equally impressive body of work."

Keanu and Schipper brainstormed possible plays for Keanu. *Caligula* by Albert Camus and *The Seagull* by Anton Chekov were considered, but Keanu's affinity for Shakespeare would result in the clear favorite: *Hamlet.* "*Hamlet* is the greatest part in western drama," Keanu enthused to *Time Out London* magazine. "It's as far as you can go as an actor with love, anger, trust, belief and spiritual anything. Hamlet is the top, constantly asking you to go further."

With initial talks going well, Schipper turned to veteran theater director Lewis Baumander, who knew Keanu well, having directed a very young Keanu in a 1985 production of *Romeo & Juliet* during Keanu's tenure at the Leah Posluns Theater School in Toronto. In the book *Keanu* by Sheila Johnston, Baumander recalled the day Keanu auditioned for *Hamlet*. "In walked Keanu with a passion, a hunger and a zeal. He told me he needed to play Mercutio. He did the Queen Mab speech and was extraordinary. Only two or three times in my life have I cast someone on the spot. But I did it with Keanu."

But Keanu was still being stealth. He did not tell Schipper about the big money movie opportunities he had turned down. Schipper would find out about *Speed 2* and, most importantly, *Heat,* on his own, as he told the *Winnipeg Free Press*. "Keanu agreed to come do *Hamlet* for scale (reportedly less than $2000 a week). I'm pretty sure he turned down around $6 million to be in *Heat*. This speaks to what an honorable person he is."

However, a Venice, California lunch meeting resulted in a moment of doubt. Schipper had always sensed that while Keanu's creative instincts were solid, there was the specter of a big bucks Hollywood offer looming on the horizon to disrupt *Hamlet*. "During that final pitch, Keanu was still very interested," he told the *Winnipeg Free Press*. "But, at one point, he asked how much time he would have to give notice if a really big film offer came up. I said then say no now. If you say yes and we promise you to our audience, then you can't no later. If you say yes, than you have to follow through."

Keanu said yes.

The run up to *Hamlet* was like a shakedown cruise in which Keanu spent five weeks in intense rehearsal, getting to know his castmates and, above all, learning and memorizing the estimated 1,500 lines of dialogue. For Keanu, it was an exciting return to his acting roots in Canada and the less stressful environment of Winnipeg. Great pains were taken to shield Keanu from the prying eyes of the press in the weeks leading up to the five-week run of *Hamlet*. Only a handful of interviews, with primarily Canadian press, were allowed. And upon penalty of death, a stringent no taping policy for any of the performances was enforced. For his part, Keanu was moving easily through the city, often spotted going in and out of local restaurants and clubs. He was accommodating when recognized and approached, signing the occasional autograph and posing for photos. But beneath the surface, there was the Keanu who was mentally focused on the task at hand, which was proving that there was more to Keanu than mere Hollywood action stud.

Word soon got out that Keanu was doing *Hamlet* in Winnipeg and the mania began. Stories began to emerge about rabid fans from around the world converging on Winnipeg. A group of women on holiday from Japan bought tickets for 10 consecutive performances while one enterprising Australian woman managed tickets to eight shows and would hang around Winnipeg for an entire month hoping for a Keanu encounter.

Speculation ran rampant on opening night. Would Keanu prove to the world that he was a stage savvy actor fully capable of tackling the bard or would he fall flat and limp back to the safety net of big paychecks in Hollywood? As the curtain went up, it remained to be seen.

Over the course of five weeks, Keanu seemed to have proved his point. His mastery of *Hamlet* was ambitious in tone and execution. Keanu was raw in the role, by turns, according to critics, a bit strident and overwrought, but those minor critiques were more than balanced by the drive and intensity Keanu brought to the role. And at the end of his run in *Hamlet,* Keanu would prove his true mettle of an actor in search of bigger and better challenges. Keanu emerged mentally and emotionally triumphant and satisfied that he had done right by the legendary and ambitious role.

"Shakespeare is physically thrilling," he told *Macleans*. "It goes to my brain and into my heart."

CHAPTER SIXTEEN
KEANU GIVES IT AWAY

By the mid '90s, consensus was that Keanu was a very rich man. Not that he was suddenly presenting himself as a man of wealth and taste; the actor still dressed and acted as a man of the people, even one who was just getting by.

But while nobody was willing to do more than speculate on the dollars and cents of Keanu, turning down a reported $20 million dollars total to do *Speed 2* and *Heat* had to tell the world something. Like just about everything in Keanu's world, he was mum about his bank balance though he would occasionally, often good-naturedly, refer to the question of money.

"Money is the last thing I think about," he told *Hello Magazine*. "I could live on what I've already made for the next few centuries." In a similar moment he explained to *Hollywood.com* that "Money doesn't mean anything to me. I've made a lot of money but I want to enjoy life and not stress myself building my bank account." In yet another telling comment, Keanu described the never-ending interest in his net worth and lifestyle when he told *Hollywood.com,* "I give lots of money away and live simply."

Not surprisingly, Keanu has proven quite the

philanthropist, regularly funding or making generous donations to *Stand Up To Cancer*, *Sick Kids* (a teaching hospital in Toronto), *PETA* and *SCORE* (an organization dealing with the care and treatment of hockey players who have suffered spinal cord injuries). Keanu has also been known to show up at charity call-in fund drives and take phone calls. That most of his good works have gone largely little noticed by the media is in line with the actor's stealth approach to giving, as he explained in an interview with *Ladies Home Journal*. "I don't like to attach my names to things. I just let the foundations do what they do."

Keanu is well known for putting his money where his art is, even to help the cause of projects he's involved with. A case in point was the 1997 film *The Devil's Advocate*. Pacino was interested in playing the lead in the legal/horror mashup. The only problem? Pacino's asking price was too steep for the film's budget. In stepped Keanu, who offered to cut $2 million off his own salary so that the film could afford to land Pacino. Keanu's reasoning was simple. He had always admired Pacino and was champing at the bit to be in a film with him. The money sacrificed would be worth it for the opportunity to play opposite a legend.

"There's not enough I can say about his acting," Keanu gushed about Pacino in *TV Week*. "He's the man."

The same reasoning was behind his participation in the sports/comedy *The Replacements* (2000). Gene Hackman was up for the lead, but his fee was too much for the budget to handle. In this instance, Keanu stepped up in a big way, giving up fully 90 percent of his salary to appear opposite the legendary actor. "I got to work with Gene Hackman," said Keanu in a conversation with *Zap2It.com*. "That was one of the best things that ever happened to me."

But that largess pales by comparison to the generosity Keanu rained down on *The Matrix* (1999), which has become something of an urban legend to be either believed or denied.

The reality is that Keanu received $10 million up front for the first *Matrix* film, plus 10 percent of any back end profits, which increased Keanu's take to an estimated $35 million. When he re-upped to appear in the second and third installments of *The Matrix* trilogy, he received $15 million up front for each of those films, plus 15 percent of back end profits. So far so good. But what has been wildly reported by such media outlets as *The Wall Street Journal* and *ABC News* is that upon signing that second deal, Keanu immediately gave an estimated $75 million of his portion of the deal to the special effects team, effectively turning each FX member into an instant millionaire.

This is where things get a bit iffy.

UPROXX.com has reported that members of the effects team have claimed they never received a check from Keanu or any money connected to Keanu's alleged generosity. Still, the legend continues to hang around and adds fuel to the notion of Keanu as a generous so-and-so. And as it turned out, in a Hollywood business sort of way, he really was. The reality was that Keanu did, in fact, take a percentage of his back-end deal and put it into the budget of the second and third film in order to keep the FX people working effectively on the effects-heavy films.

Because, to Keanu's way of thinking, they were the real stars of *The Matrix* films.

CHAPTER SEVENTEEN
KEANU'S DARK DAYS

Jennifer Syme left her hometown of Pico Rivera, California at age 18. Destination: Los Angeles. Her future plans were unclear. It was whatever happened next.

Syme was alternately shy and modest, yet quietly determined. She was determined to somehow, some way make a name for herself in the entertainment business. The teen was a people person, a natural networker. She would use those talents to land an assistant's job with filmmaker David Lynch not long after she hit Hollywood. She did a couple of small roles in two of Lynch's films. Syme also found her way into the celebrity party circuit, not as a groupie, but as somebody who used the party atmosphere to get to know people and allow people to know her.

At several of these parties, she made the acquaintance of Karen Reeves, Keanu's sister, and the pair formed a strong social relationship. So much so that when they both ended up at a record company promotional party for Keanu's band Dogstar in 1998, Karen offered to introduce Jennifer to her brother.

Keanu had reached a stage in his life when professional considerations would often be overlapped by

95

personal desires. He was seemingly never without female companionship, but when asked, he would grow wistful at the prospect of settling into a stable relationship and having a family. When he was introduced to Syme, Keanu was almost immediately smitten.

"In 1998, I met Jennifer," he was quoted in an *MSN.com* article. "We fell instantly in love."

According to subsequent media reports "instantly" may have been a bit of an exaggeration. But not by much. Keanu was immediately attracted to her modesty and determination. What was described in *MSN.com* as "a slow and casual development of a relationship" was, in reality, a lightning-fast progression to being lovers. In August 1999, the couple went public with the announcement that Jennifer was pregnant with Keanu's child.

Keanu was over the moon with joy. So much so that those who knew Keanu well were shocked when Keanu did a very un-Keanu kind of thing. He bought a house specifically for Syme and the baby to live. Keanu and Syme were in bliss.

Their relationship continued to be one that was unorthodox by most standards. They were not living together during the pregnancy and, according to reports, had no intention of getting married. And to many, there seemed nothing wrong with that. Former girlfriend Jenny Rose was one of those who sprang to the defense of their lifestyle. In a conversation with *New Weekly Magazine*, she said, "All (Jennifer) wants is for Keanu to be a good father to her baby. Others might call it flaky or weird but to Keanu and Jennifer, it's fine to have a baby and not be married."

The ensuing months were happy and chaotic. Keanu was constantly working and away from Syme often. But they were constantly in touch, sharing the small but exciting moments of her pregnancy and upcoming parenthood. Keanu would regularly go on solo shopping trips and return with gifts for mother and baby. When it was discovered that they were having a girl, Jennifer and Keanu were quick to give the child a name, Ava Archer Reeves.

Keanu was intent on being the best father he could possibly be and, as he offered in *Now Magazine,* with good reason. "I want to be a part of their (Jennifer and Ava) life. My dad walked out on me so I know what it's like to grow up without a father. I wouldn't ever do that to my child."

Everything was going well with the pregnancy throughout the year. But in late December, Syme felt there was something wrong. It had been several days since she had felt any movement from the baby. With Keanu, she went to her doctor, who performed an ultrasound. On December 24, mere days before Jennifer was due to give birth, the baby was pronounced stillborn. According to various media reports, Keanu held his girlfriend close. When they were given the sad news they both cried.

Ava Archer Reeves was buried at The Westwood Village Memorial Park in Los Angeles. A simple marker read Ava Archer Reeves and the date of her birth and death as 1999. Keanu and Syme's grief was palpable.

The grief continued to eat at Keanu and Syme's relationship, which quickly succumbed to the couple's inability to openly express what they were feeling. Years later, Keanu would recall those painful last days of their relationship. In an interview with *Parade* magazine, he said, "Grief changes shape but it never ends. People have a misconception of how to deal with grief. They say 'It's done and I'm better.' They're wrong."

Sadly, the strain of loss would be too much, and Keanu and Syme eventually parted ways. They vowed to remain friends, and Keanu would continue to offer financial support. But for all intents and purposes, the love was gone. Keanu would lose himself in his work, most notably *The Matrix*. Jennifer did not have it so easy, her main companions being loneliness and depression, for which she was being treated with prescription drugs. She would soon turn to alcohol and return to the partying lifestyle.

On April 1, 2001, Keanu and Syme were spotted having brunch together at the restaurant Crepes on Cole in San Francisco. The next morning, Keanu was awakened by a hysterical, sobbing phone call from Jennifer's mother. Her daughter was dead. Shaken by the news, Keanu immediately called the Los Angeles County Coroner's Office and, according to a report filed by *People* magazine, stammered, "Is Jennifer Syme there?"

She was.

According to countless media reports that included the *New York Post* and *People*, Jennifer had been at a party thrown by shock rocker Marilyn Manson. At one point in the evening, Jennifer was driven home by a designated driver. Sometime around 6 a.m., Syme had reportedly decided she wanted to return to the party, climbed into her Jeep Cherokee and was driving erratically down Cahuenga Boulevard when she sideswiped three parked cars and rolled over several times. Syme was thrown from the car and died instantly.

As with any celebrity passing, Syme's death would bring accusations and lawsuits. Of the latter, Syme r's mother felt that Marilyn Manson had been a contributing factor in her daughter's death. Through all the legal wrangling, Keanu would be conspicuous by his absence. Syme would be buried in a plot next to daughter Ava at Westwood Village Memorial Park. Keanu was there, barely keeping it together, emotionally shut down, for a time, he was in seclusion, not talking or seeing anyone. Eventually he would come out of his shell and return to his professional life. But it was plain that the hurt still lingered. The 18 months that had brought more tragedy than most could bear would follow Keanu for the rest of his days.

Over the years, it would become gradually easier to talk about the deaths of Jennifer and Ava. But it was something that still haunted him, and even attempting to open up about it would see Keanu visibly in agony. Such was the case in 2006, when he confessed his feelings to *Parade*.

"I miss being a part of their lives and them being a part of mine. I wonder what the present would be like if they were here, what we might have done together. I miss all the great things that will never be."

For Keanu, the days and months would pass. Slowly the phone began to ring. Friends were calling and checking on how he was doing. The darkness and the sadness were still in his private thoughts. But there were the occasional glimpses of light as Keanu fought back against the twin tragedies that had impacted his life.

"I think after loss, life requires an act of reclaiming," Keanu told *Parade*. "You have to reject being overwhelmed. Life has to go on."

CHAPTER EIGHTEEN
THE MATRIX KICKS KEANU'S ASS

Keanu was going through a bit of a mid-life crisis going into late 1997.

He had arrived on the Hollywood scene, but to the important decision makers and observers, he was not quite there. He had been in big commercial blockbusters and filmmakers were beating down his door with scripts. But there were intangibles that seemed to linger, doubts that he had not truly become the go-to guy. He had done quality small projects, such as *A Walk in the Clouds* and *Feeling Minnesota*, that, despite giving him street cred as a highly talented actor, also gave Hollywood the nagging impression that, career-wise, he was still unfocused. They wanted a cookie-cutter actor who they could plug into a niche and watch him connect the dots. And Keanu was not that cat.

But he was definitely *almost* there and one of the first signs of coming greatness would be *The Matrix,* a massive, special-effects heavy, technology-laden look into a future in which a techno nerd named Neo embarks on an action-packed journey to discover truth and untruth in an insulated and often corrupt time. Featuring aspects of futuristic martial arts-style fighting and a hero of a few words, *The Matrix* had all the makings of either a monster success or a colossal bomb. In other words, something that was right up Keanu's alley.

But was it?

For somebody who would be tasked with projecting a believable character in a technologically advanced future, Keanu, by his own admission, was still a primitive to the extreme, as he offered in an interview with *Parade*. "I don't own a computer and I don't email. I'm fascinated by people who freak out when they don't get an instant response to an email."

At the moment it did not matter that Keanu could not talk the talk because he was at the end of a particularly long line of A-list actors who were being offered the role of Neo ahead of him.

Will Smith was offered the role but turned it down because he did not understand the concept, opting for the simpler *The Wild Wild West*. In no particular order, Brad Pitt, Val Kilmer and Nicolas Cage all said thanks but no thanks. At one point, the idea was floated to make Neo female, and the project was offered to Sandra Bullock, who gracefully declined.

Finally, it boiled down to a battle of wills between the studio and the directors. The directors, the Wachowski brothers, wanted Johnny Depp. The studio wanted Keanu. The studio won which, in hindsight, was the right choice because, in his often naïve/simplistic way, Keanu seemed to have an innate feel for the film and character shortly after reading a very early draft of the script for the first time.

"When I read the script, it made my blood happy," Keanu said in a *Wired* feature. Keanu would be more succinct on the subject in conversation with *The Morning Call*. "I think the movie asks the question 'What is truth?'

Keanu would quickly discover that the Wachowski brothers were not fooling around with yet another variation on simplistic comic book action. This was serious business, and it became even more serious when, upon officially being accepted as Neo, Reeves and other members of the cast were given a laundry list of "out there" literature that they would have to read and understand before they could read the shooting draft of the script. The heavy reading included *Simulacra and Simulation, Out of Control: The New Biology of Machines, Social Systems and the Economic World* and Dylan Evans' theories on *Psychological Evolution.*

In the *Wired* piece, Keanu gleefully recalled his marching orders from the directors. "They just said 'go read and see what it is.' For me, it was just fun reading."

Potentially less fun was the marathon of a shooting schedule that *The Matrix* would entail: Four months of non-stop martial arts training for the ambitious action sequences and stunts plus an additional eight months of actual filming.

Keanu was fine with that. "They told me they wanted me to train for four months prior to filming and I got a big grin on my face and said yes," he told *Wired.* In the same article the Wachowski's related how they felt when Keanu agreed. "We knew it would take a maniacal commitment from someone. And we knew Keanu was our maniac."

Keanu was not fine with what happened one morning shortly before the start of the training.

"I have a two level fusion," Keanu playing doctor told *Rolling Stone.* "I had one old compressed disc and one shattered disc. One of them was 10 years old and, eventually, one started sticking to my spinal cord. I found myself starting to fall over in the shower in the morning because I was losing my sense of balance."

Keanu was examined by his doctor and the prognosis was dire.

He had to have an operation to fuse the two vertebrate or he would risk becoming a quadriplegic. Keanu went under the knife. Keanu had barely emerged from the successful surgery when he was thrust into what would be the physical torment of *The Matrix*. Already a groundbreaking film on several fronts, the Wachowski directors had something different in mind for the ambitious fighting sequences.

Rather than substitute stunt people for the actors in pivotal scenes, it was decided that the actors would do all the fight scenes themselves, Hong Kong kung fu style. The directors approached legendary Hong Kong fight choreographer Yuen Woo Ping with the proposal that he train all the lead actors over a four-month period prior to the start of production. For Ping, it was a challenge he had never faced, and he was initially reluctant to take on what he knew would be a massive undertaking. Ultimately, he would agree to train the actors, which put Keanu right in the firing line.

Keanu was conspicuous by the neck brace he would wear during the first two months of pre-production training. But from the first day he was nothing if not determined, more than willing to put in 10-hour days as Ping put him through endless and strenuous fighting moves and wire work sequences.

Ping had decided that the best approach to the training would be to tailor each actor's movements to their real attributes. In Keanu, he saw diligence.

Keanu's first months of training would be determined by his post-operation condition. At first, his practice sessions were limited to less strenuous moves and no kicks, an element that would be evident in the film, when Keanu does very few kicks on-screen.

The training was largely a harrowing emotional experience as Keanu attempted to balance the physical and emotional side of attempting rigorous stunts while still being on the mend. "The hard part is that my body wanted to go further and faster," he told *Wired*, "and my will but it was all being checked by my neck and the fear that came with it."

But Keanu persisted and would ultimately receive high marks from the directors and the kung fu coordinator. The Wachowski brothers acknowledged in the now out-of-print *Martialarm Martial Arts* magazine that "Keanu understood why it (the training) was necessary and the dedication it required." Coordinator Ping, in the same interview, said "Keanu was very dedicated to doing his kung fu and serious about his job. He's a perfectionist."

Interestingly, Keanu's physical limitations would prove helpful. When he would turn his head during the execution of a move, his shoulders and chest would follow because of his limited flexibility, a situation that, on screen, would add a sense of dynamic to Neo's fighting movements.

The impact of what Keanu was doing became a bigger reality once production on *The Matrix* began in earnest. The film was now officially on the clock and everybody, including Keanu, knew the clock was ticking at an unforgiving pace.

Keanu was still suffering some discomfort from his

surgery. So many of the high-energy action sequences that were planned to be filmed early on were rescheduled to the latter part of the shoot. Which Keanu, ever the perfectionist, found frustrating. So much so that when he failed to perform a triple kick during one fight scene, he insisted that the scene be reshot. The second time around proved the charm, and three days later, the scene was nailed in a mere three takes. Keanu's willingness to go the extra mile to make *The Matrix* work was much in evidence during the filming of a pivotal scene, a cellphone conversation between Neo and Morpheus. Keanu insisted he could climb up the window 34 floors high without the aid of a stuntman. The entire crew held their collective breath and Keanu made like Spiderman and lived to tell about it.

Keanu's willingness to do whatever it took was a constant source of enjoyment and encouragement as *The Matrix* rounded into its final days of shooting. The handling of one scene in particular would serve to drive that point home.

For the early-in-the film sequence in which Neo emerges from the pod into the real world, the script described Neo as thin, gaunt and hairless, perhaps a faint homage to the star child at the conclusion of *2001: A Space Odyssey*. Initially, the directors thought in terms of an elaborate makeup job. But in conversation with Keanu, both sides agreed that the method approach would better serve the tone of the movie.

And so, several days before the scene was to be shot, Keanu went on a crash diet that shed 15 pounds. On the day of the filming, crew members were surprised and just a bit taken aback when they spotted Keanu naked in a bathtub, razor in hand, shaving off his head and body hair. Reports were that Keanu looked so stark and otherworldly as he walked onto the set that even the most non-plussed in the crowd had a hard time looking him in the eye. He looked that strange.

And the strangeness would follow him after the conclusion of filming. Dogstar was scheduled to play a gig in Los Angeles and Keanu was very much in his *Matrix* look. His hair had barely begun to grow back and his body was still looking emaciated. Rock stars are notorious for appearing unhealthy. But Keanu on stage, his bass slung low, his face distorted in emotion, looked downright alien. All of which translated into concern on the part of fans, who mistook Keanu's look as actual illness. It would take a while, but Keanu would eventually fill out into his normal Keanu physique. But one thing was certain: he had gone toe to toe with *The Matrix* and had emerged victorious. As always, the recovery time was short and Keanu was looking for something totally out of character for his next project. He found it in a modestly budgeted supernatural thriller entitled *The Gift*, in which Keanu willingly played the totally unsympathetic role of an abusive redneck husband. "One of my ambitions as an actor is to try and play different kinds of parts," he told *Blue Magazine*. I liked my character in *The Gift*. I liked his intensity."

Keanu would go all Method in getting the character of Donnie Barksdale right, arriving at the southern location weeks early, getting an old, beat-up truck and riding around to local redneck bars in an attempt to get the accent right and figure out the ins and outs of redneck culture. When it came time to begin filming, director Sam Rami had his own ideas about how to bring authenticity to the abusive relationship between Keanu's character and actress Hilary Swank, who played his wife.

Rami set up an improvisation scene in a small room where the actors acted out an argument that quickly escalated from name-calling to physical violence. At one point, the director instructed Keanu to hit his wife every time he called her a name. Keanu the actor was very much into the moment, striking Swank as he screamed, and at one point, shoving her violently against a wall and taking her clothes off. The improvisation was emotionally cathartic for both actors, but for Keanu was particularly taxing.

"I could never imagine being that violent in real life," he said in a *Blue* conversation. "I never have hit a woman. I remember coming out of the improvisation and my heart was racing and everything got really quiet. "I felt changed. I felt like I had crossed a boundary."

CHAPTER NINETEEN
KEANU GETS SCREWED

It goes without saying that Keanu is generous to a fault. By the year 2000, he was seemingly everywhere, addressing personal and professional needs in big and small moments. But Keanu's playground, being Hollywood aka Jaws, it was inevitable that a good deed would come back and bite him.

Keanu had been good friends with Joe Charbanic since his early hockey days in Los Angeles. Charbanic had been struggling on the fringes of the movie biz for years, working to little acclaim as a music video producer for artists including *311*, *Slash* and Alicia Keys, and he'd logged some time on the road with Dogstar during their touring days. By 2000, Charbanic seemed poised to break into the big time as a first-time film director with a gritty little thriller called *The Watcher,* in which a cop and a serial killer go at each other as the body count rises. All he needed was an actor of note to play the killer. He turned to Keanu for help.

"I never found the script that interesting," Keanu told the *Calgary Sun*. But he was struck by the independent, arty feel of the production and the opportunity to play a villain. And, of course, there was the opportunity to help out an old friend. Keanu agreed

109

to do a handful of days on the film for the actor's union minimum standard pay (roughly $1,000 a day), a far cry from the $15 million he was pulling down as his going rate for films like *The Matrix*. Keanu knew his management would not be thrilled, so he went behind their backs and agreed to do the film.

What happened next is open to some speculation. It was assumed that somewhere in the negotiations, Keanu signed some kind of deal document. Assumed being the watchword here, because, as reported in the *Calgary Sun* 2001, Keanu almost matter-of-factly acknowledged "A friend of mine forged my signature on the agreement."

Nevertheless, Keanu had given his word and had agreed to do the film. What he was not aware of was that shortly after he had signed on to the project, the producers of *The Watcher*, as reported by the *London Evening Standard,* immediately flew to Europe and dangled Keanu's attachment to the film in front of investors, who added an additional $30 million to the film's budget.

The influx of money suddenly turned *The Watcher* into a much bigger movie than Keanu had envisioned. Rather than a small indie-style film in which Keanu's serial killer made only token appearances, the concept and script were suddenly expanded to make Keanu's character a lead role with much more screen time and an increased total of 14 shooting days. Adding insult to injury, the additional funds allowed the producers to go out and hire his co-stars, James Spader and Marisa Tomei, at salaries much higher than Keanu's.

Director Charbanic essentially admitted as much in interviews with the *Chicago Sun Times* and the *London Evening Standard*. "The script did change. It

110

got bigger than Keanu wanted. He wanted it to be a little boutique film. He had liked the original film because it allowed him to be the bad guy."

The normally good-natured Keanu suddenly morphed into a real bad guy, making threatening noises about pulling out of the film. It was then that he was forced to learn a hard Hollywood lesson. Whether Keanu actually signed the contract or a mysterious and never-disclosed assistant had forged his signature, the fact remained that a contract with his name on it was valid, binding, and did not offer any legal way out for the actor without resulting in a protracted and expensive legal battle.

Keanu would finally throw up his hands. "I couldn't prove that he (his assistant) had forged my signature and I didn't want to get sued, so I had no other choice but to do the film," he told the *Calgary Sun*.

Not surprisingly, the vibe on the set of *The Watcher* was tense on a number of levels. The relationship between Keanu and his one-time good buddy Charbanic was essentially over and, although he remained a total professional on the set, they were now barely speaking. The same was true of Keanu and his co-stars who, according to reports, were now making as much as half a million more than he was. The conclusion of filming should have been the end of a very unpleasant experience for Keanu. But it than that Keanu decided to play hardball with Universal Pictures, who was releasing the film.

Keanu copped an attitude that only an actor with his kind of power could. He refused to promote the film in any way and made it very clear that if the media approached him, he would disown the movie. It did not take long for Universal to blink, and studio executives were falling all over themselves with concessions.

They agreed that his name would appear below the title on all print advertising and posters, rather than in big letters above the title. They agreed that Keanu would not appear in more than 30 percent of any promotional trailers. And finally, they were offering Keanu a reported generous slice of any profits from the film. In exchange, Keanu would refrain from talking about *The Watcher* until a year after its release.

The Watcher would open to largely negative reviews, including less-than-positive opinions regarding Keanu's ability to effectively portray a serial killer. The movie was essentially out of theaters in a scant few weeks.

Charbanic attempted an epitaph in the *London Evening Standard* when he said, "I think Keanu and I were both a little mad at each other. Every time friends get in business together, it doesn't go well. I went in a little naïve because it was my first film."

For his part, Keanu agreed to the terms of his deal with Universal. Twelve months after the release of *The Watcher*, Keanu, with tongue firmly planted in his cheek, told the *Calgary Sun* "If it's September that means it's been a year, so I can finally talk."

CHAPTER TWENTY
KEANU'S WOMEN: PART II

Following the death of Jennifer Syme, Keanu went into emotional lockdown for the better part of three years. And, as they are prone to do, the entertainment press had a field day at the expense of the actor's pain. Stories circulated that Keanu had sworn up and down that he would never marry and was gun-shy about ever having a serious relationship again.

Keanu's period of emotional isolation seemingly came to an end in 2004 when it was circulated in the tabloid press that Keanu was dating actress Claire Forlani whose credits include the motion picture *Meet Joe Black* and the television series *NCIS New York*. Typical of Hollywood relationship reporting, the reality was that the couple dated for three years. Less certain is the story that the couple broke up when Keanu reportedly proposed to the actress. When asked by the *New York Daily News*, Keanu laughed it all off by saying, "We're good friends."

That may well have been the case, because during the time Keanu and Forlani were dating, the actor was also reportedly involved with a whole bevy of other "friends." In 2005, Keanu was supposedly juggling relationships with the actresses Autumn MacIntosh and Lynn Collins, and, according to tabloid reports, was serious enough with MacIntosh to be seriously contemplating marriage. Obviously marriage was off the books, especially when that same year saw Keanu keeping serious company with actresses Diane Keaton, Kelli Garner and Hallie Myers Shyer.

Not that Keanu was being a player. When he was with a woman in anything remotely close to a relationship, the impression had always been that he was loyal and faithful, although the time between breakups and hookups often seemed seamless. When Keanu broke up with Collins—after seven months and what many speculated was his first serious relationship since the death of Jennifer—he was immediately involved with Keaton, who was 20 years his senior. Keaton was typical of Keanu's dating history, as the relationship was over the same year it started. Keanu and Hallie Meyers Shyer wound down what had reportedly been a largely clandestine relationship, and he was then briefly paired with actress Martha Higareda.

How serious Keanu was with any of these women became a good-natured game in Hollywood gossip circles. Inevitably there would be pictures to indicate romantic sparks and breathless speculation, but by the time these couplings generated any steam, they were invariably over, and Keanu was on to the next.

But in one of his more philosophical moments with *Grazia Magazine*, Keanu offered that while being around women in friendship situations was the norm for him, he was definitely a proponent of love and living happily ever after. "I think to give love and to receive love is really the nourishment in our lives. Love is very important but it also changes. To find a soul mate has been there for me for quite a while. Maybe I'll get lucky and be able to cross it off the list sooner or later."

As it turned out, later seemed to be the watchword. In 2008, Keanu continued to be active on the dating scene with real or, as interpreted by the press, imagined involvements with actress Parker Posey, a very real hot-and-heavy tryst with actress-model China Chow on the French Rivera; and what may or may not have been a cozy motorcycle ride and a dinner with British television host Trinny Woodall.

Cooler heads in the media were quick to point out that many of Keanu's romantic encounters were nothing more than business get-togethers or, as Keanu was known to say, just friends or brief encounters at parties. In any case, Keanu continued to be a hot topic when it came to his relationships, real or imagined, with women. And as his stature in the industry grew, those moments became more conspicuous by his reported coupling with A-listers in their own right.

Exhibit A: In 2009-10, Keanu had been regularly seen out and about with Cameron Diaz and Charlize Theron. But two things remained certain when it came to Keanu's reported love life during the 2000's.

One, Keanu was still single and two, Keanu was not talking. At least not much. But *Vanity Fair* put the question to him and caught him in a nostalgic frame of mind. "Unfortunately, at the moment, I'm not in a serious relationship. But you know I'm looking. It was just in the last couple of years where I was even open to the idea of being in another relationship. But it was like 'Aaggh! God, forget all that stuff. Let's just be friends.'"

CHAPTER TWENTY-ONE
KEANU ABOVE AND BELOW

Important dates to remember. *The Matrix: Reloaded* was released on May 5, 2003. *The Matrix: Revolutions* was released on November 5, 2003. Lost in the rush of hype and holler was the lesser-known fact that Keanu celebrated his 39th birthday on September 2, 2003. With no fanfare.

In fact, anyone passing through Los Angeles' Dan Tana's Restaurant that evening might well have been shocked to see Keanu alone at a corner table, eating pasta. And, according to the *WENN Syndicate*, it was not like he didn't have offers of companionship. It turns out that half a dozen glamorous models offered to help him celebrate. Keanu's response had been "I'm happy spending the big day alone."

Keanu is notorious for being a man of a few words. Whether by design or his mood at any given moment, he seems to take great delight in cutting to the quick and stating the obvious, making long monologues superfluous. Such was definitely the case when *Cosmopolitan* magazine attempted to talk up specifics on the follow-ups to *The Matrix*, *The Matrix: Reloaded* and *The Matrix: Revolutions*.

Keanu's response? "Work hard. Play hard."

The long and short of it was actually this. The success of *The Matrix* spurred an immediate call for a follow up. But rather than one film, filmmakers and the bottom-line conscious studio decided that it would make perfect sense to film *The Matrix: Reloaded* and *The Matrix: Revolutions* back to back. The logistics would be staggering. Training and the actual filming would take 22 months and entail a three-year commitment by Keanu. Was he up to the task? You betcha.

The massive box office and critical success of the two sequels served their purpose on a whole lot of levels, the most obvious being that, after flirting with the notion of being a commercial film superstar for years, *The Matrix* trilogy would put Keanu over the top.

Or perhaps *back* on top.

Observers of the business side of Hollywood were quick to note that Keanu had been in a bit of a dollars-and-cents slump with *The Watcher*, *Sweet November* and *The Replacements* earning negative reviews and only modest box office success. Not that the failures were necessarily Keanu's fault, but the reality was that it was his name on the marquee that was considered to be box office gold. Anything less and the actor was suddenly suspect. Happily, *The Matrix* trilogy had given Keanu back his mojo.

So now what? Keanu promptly signed a three-picture deal with Warner Bros., worth a reported $75 million. He had more scripts to consider than he could possibly do in a lifetime. And, in typical Keanu fashion, he was in no hurry to do much of anything.

"I can't control who hires me," he told *United Press International*. "But I do know that I need to do a play. I want to do a play. I've got to get back on stage because I love it."

Keanu conceded that the success of *The Matrix* films had put him in rarified state as it pertained to Hollywood's perception of him. But he couched his current state in deeper philosophical tones in an article in *The Times*. "It's not really a sense of relief. It's kind of a new life personally and professionally. All of a sudden it's like 'What do I do now? Who am I now?' The work on *The Matrix* films defined my life for the better part of three years. Right now, it's like that ship has sailed. But we're still waiting to see where it goes."

Keanu would also address his personal state of mind in the wake of *The Matrix* films in conversation with *Handbag.com*. "I don't feel as much of a loner as I used to. I feel much more present and open as a human being. I'm also less anguished."

So much so that the notoriously nomadic Keanu, who has seemingly spent his entire Hollywood life living out of hotels and short-term rentals, finally took the grown-up plunge of buying a home in Hollywood for a reported $5 million. For Keanu, it was simply the right move at the right time. He had recently turned 40, was settled in his level of stardom and in need of some roots.

"There were many years where I led a bit of a gypsy life," he told *Brampton Guardian.com*. "I worked and then came back to Los Angeles. I rented houses. After a while, I felt I wanted to buy a home. And so for a couple of years I went looking. And then you walk into a place and go 'This is it, this is it!' It gives you something. It's a safe place, a place to rest, a place to think, a place to entertain. It's great to have it."

Putting down roots may have given him comfort, but over the next couple years, Keanu would remain eccentric and selective in his choice of films. *Something's Gotta Give*, a big, splashy romantic comedy involving a love triangle, was safe, commercially viable big-studio stuff. Which was something that Keanu had become less and less averse to in the wake of his *Matrix* blockbusters. Throw in co-stars Jack Nicholson and Diane Keaton and it gave the actor a wind-down vehicle following the years of special effects and action.

Keanu's decision to do *Something's Gotta Give* was simple. "It basically boiled down to the question of where there is some good work to be had," he offered *Beliefnet.com*. "I wanted to act. With *Something's Gotta Give*, I liked the people involved and it was a really good role. Light romantic comedy was something I hadn't done in a while."

But Keanu's love of all things fantastic could not keep him grounded in reality for too long. The next stop would be the movie version of the popular horror comic book *Hellblazer* called *Constantine*. The storyline follows Constantine, a cynical, burned-out occult detective whose youthful suicide attempt has put him in a bad place with heaven. In an attempt to seek salvation, Constantine, with the power to communicate with both angels and demons, finds demons and sends them back to hell.

Keanu had received the script while doing *The Matrix* sequels and it immediately appealed to him on a lot of levels. "I liked the idea of the character," he explained to *IndieLondon.com*. "I liked this hard edged, hard boiled, fatalistic, cynical, smug, trapped, cursed thing. I like the idea that he basically gives the finger to the devil."

Following *Constantine*, Keanu was definitely feeling it was time for a change. "I didn't hope to repeat myself," he told *Female.com*. "I just wanted to deal with a kind of naturalistic piece for a change." He found exactly that in a miniscule independent film called *Thumbsucker*, a dramatic comedy that focused on the trials of a 17-year-old boy dealing with a lifelong thumb-sucking habit, romance and ADHD. *Thumbsucker's* $3 million budget was light years removed from Keanu's salary demands, but the actor was drawn to the quality of the writing and the humanity. For his three days of work on the film, Keanu portrayed Dr. Perry Lyman, a New Age orthodontist with underlying issues of his own.

Ellie Parker, featuring Naomi Watts, is an ironic bit of business. Originally a 16-minute short released briefly in 2001, this tale of the life and loves of an actress trying to make it in Hollywood was lengthened to feature length and finally released in 2005. It is total art house, hand-held camera work and was shot on video. In it, Keanu plays a cameo as Keanu in a short concert segment from his Dogstar days. And, in a segment left over from the original short, Keanu's late girlfriend Jennifer Syme plays a character called Casting Chick. *Ellie Parker* had a very minor theatrical release and then disappeared into the void. That Keanu has barely acknowledged the film over the years most likely has to do with the fact that he, indirectly, shares screen time with the late love of his life.

During this period of Keanu being creatively all over the place, the actor once again took a flyer at music, playing bass in another local Los Angeles band called Becky. Keanu managed to juggle Becky and his movie career for about a year and thoroughly enjoyed playing music again. But the same conflict of interest quickly got in the way. "I was playing with Becky for about a year," he told *Contactmusic.com*. "But they wanted to get record deals and go on tour and I couldn't do that so I bowed out."

It was shortly before leaving Becky that Keanu arrived—in the traditional Hollywood sense—when, on January 31, 2005, he joined the pantheon of legends inducted into the Hollywood Walk of Fame. Beaming brightly and thanking everybody as his star was unveiled at 6801 Hollywood Boulevard, Keanu was sincere in accepting the honor. As much as he poo-pooed much of Hollywood tradition, he knew in his gut that…

…That star in the sidewalk meant he had truly arrived.

CHAPTER TWENTY-TWO
THE MISADVENTURES OF KEANU

When Keanu decides to take to the streets of Los Angeles on his motorcycle, he tends to follow the rules of the road... For the most part. "I only drive in Los Angeles without a helmet when the police aren't looking," he explained to *IndieLondon*. "It's just about not getting caught. It's not like I have a special 'I'm a famous guy' pass."

And he would hint as much some years later while promoting his gritty crime/cop drama *Street Kings* in conversation with *Indie London*. "Generally, I'm treated the same as everybody else by the cops. I have never really had a bad experience with the police. Well that's not true. I was put in handcuffs once. But that was probably my own fault. I just didn't say 'yes sir, no sir' quickly enough."

But while Keanu is, at heart, an upstanding, law-abiding citizen, there have been those moments when the actor and L.A.'s finest have crossed paths. In 1991-92, the *National Enquirer* and *Woman's Day Magazine* revealed that Keanu was stopped on three different occasions for driving on a suspended license. Logic would indicate that the police would not have discovered the suspended license issue unless they had first pulled him over for something else.

That something else may well have been what was ultimately Keanu's legendary encounter with the law when, on May 5, 1993, he was spotted driving through Los Angeles streets in an erratic manner and pulled over by the police, who immediately discovered that Keanu was intoxicated and driving under the influence. During the investigation, Keanu had a resisting arrest charge tacked on for good measure when he attempted to walk away from the scene and had to be restrained by officers. Faced with the fact that he had been caught in the act, Keanu confessed to driving under the influence, was immediately put in cuffs, taken to jail and booked, leading to a now-infamous mugshot of the actor staring drunkenly into the camera. Keanu was subsequently released and no charges were filed.

In the aftermath of that arrest, stories circulated that Keanu had allegedly been so mortified by the experience that he largely gave up his reckless ways.

In 2004, Keanu would be the classic example of being in the wrong place at the wrong time. As reported by the *SFGate.com*, Keanu was shopping at a Los Angeles supermarket when suddenly shots rang out, shattering the store's windows. Shoppers screamed. Keanu, in the finest tradition of *Speed*, yelled above the panicked customers to get down. Once the shooting stopped, Keanu found the storeowner and told him to call 911. The LAPD quickly arrived and it was determined that the drive-by had been a random shooting by a gang member. And Keanu emerged as one cool cat.

But that would not be the end of Keanu's cop

encounters. In 2006, he would be stopped and ticketed for running a red light. And there was more to come. He would sheepishly concede in a *Stern* magazine interview, "Needless to say, I've had some speeding tickets. Once I was caught going 180 in a place where the speed limit was 110."

On March 19, 2007, Keanu was driving his Porsche down the Sunset Strip when he noticed that he was being followed. He continued to drive. The car behind him continued to follow. Thirty minutes later, Keanu pulled up at a Los Angeles medical facility. He was there to visit a family friend. As he entered the facility, he noticed the car was also there. Keanu sensed that he had been followed by a paparazzo who had spotted him in Hollywood and had followed him, looking for a photographic score.

Sometime later, Keanu's unease was confirmed when, upon leaving the medical facility, he came face to face with paparazzo Alison Silva snapping away. Keanu got into his car, moved forward and turned around to leave, only to find Silva now standing in front of his car, continuing to shoot pictures. Keanu reportedly inched his car forward in an attempt to move the cameraman out of the way. Suddenly Silva went down in a heap, screaming in pain and yelling that Keanu had deliberately hit him with his car. Keanu reportedly stopped and came to the paparazzo's aid. Police and rescue units were called. Keanu gave his side of the story to authorities as Silva was taken by ambulance to a hospital.

Silva would subsequently file a lawsuit against Keanu, charging that he had deliberately rammed his car into him, causing shock and serious physical injuries. The pap demanded $711,974 in damages. The suit, filed with the Los Angeles Superior Court, would take a year and a half to make its way to trial, during which time Silva would make countless public demands of Keanu.

When the case finally came to trail, as reported by the likes of *The Los Angeles Times*, *The Huffington Post*, *USA Today* and the *New York Daily News*, Keanu would spend five days in court, often spotted signing autographs in the courthouse hallways during breaks in the trial, listening to the case against him and testifying on the stand in his defense. When it came time for him to testify, Keanu spent one hour on the stand, telling his side of the incident.

As reported by the *New York Daily News*, during his testimony Keanu would occasionally come across with humor when questioned, but primarily stuck to the facts as he saw them. "It's common sense to get out of the way when someone starts a car," he acknowledged. "I slowly moved my car forward to nudge Silva out of the way but, to my recollection, I didn't hit him. I saw his legs cross and he started to kind of stumble."

Silva's accusations would slowly crumble in the face of his inconsistent statements and what he had told the police at the accident scene. The jury would deliberate only one hour before coming back with a "not guilty" verdict.

Keanu had always been friendly and accommodating to fans who had approached him in his daily life which, in hindsight, may well have encouraged some to cross personal boundaries. At least, as reported over the years, the actor had never had a serious problem with stalkers. But all of that changed in 2014, when, in a matter of days, Keanu's home was invaded by two overzealous and most likely unhinged fans.

As reported in *The Wrap. Entertainment Tonight*, *ArizonaCentral.com* and *ENews.com*, the unusual twofer went like this:

In the first instance, Keanu awoke at 4 a.m. to the sound of noises coming from his library. He found a 40-year-old woman sitting inside. During a short conversation with the woman, she confessed that she was there to meet him rather than rob him. Keanu calmly called 911, the police arrived and the woman was taken into custody and given a psychological examination. Keanu was out of town on the second break-in when he received a phone call from his cleaning crew that they had found a naked woman on his property, and that she had taken a shower and was currently skinny-dipping in his swimming pool. The woman had apparently gotten into the house by way of a door that had been left unlocked by the cleaning crew. As with the first intruder, Keanu called 911 and the resulting arrest also resulted in a psych exam.

Ever the understated optimist, Keanu summed up the twin break-ins this way. "I had an interesting weekend but everybody's okay. All's well that ends well."

CHAPTER TWENTY-THREE
KEANU IS LOW KEY

It was midway through the 2000's and Keanu was in the mood to take some out-of-the-box chances rather than accept scripts that played to his perceived stereotype and would pay him a lot of money.

The chance-taking kicked off in a challenging way when he agreed to voice two characters in *A Scanner Darkly*, an extremely low budget animated take on legendary science fiction writer Philip K. Dick's seminal novel. Keanu enjoyed the experience of this different kind of filmmaking. Unfortunately *A Scanner Darkly* fell victim to inconsistent/amateurish animation that necessitated reshoots and a delay in filming. By that time, the movie was doomed to inconsistent reviews, a miniscule release and the tag of "commercial failure."

The opportunity to reunite with longtime friend Sandra Bullock resulted in his participation in *The Lake House*, an Americanized version of the South Korean film *Il Mare*, which centered on two star-crossed lovers whose relationship grows through a series of letters left in a mail box over the years. The professional reunion of two old friends struck the appropriate emotional tone and *The Lake House*, mixed reviews and all, went on to become an international commercial hit.

Keanu's always present social conscience and seemingly wide-ranging religious interests led to what many consider a questionable choice at best, the documentary film *The Great Warming*. The film, narrated by Keanu and singer Alanis Morrissette, attempted to meld the science-centered concept of climate warming with the philosophical evangelist faith. The result was uneven and seemingly at odds with itself.

It was at that point that Keanu suddenly found himself out on parole from 20th Century Fox's movie jail. In the ensuing years, a new regime had taken over at the studio, one seemingly inclined to welcome Keanu back in the fold. His get-out-of-jail-free card was a reimaging of the science fiction classic *The Day the Earth Stood Still*.

Keanu was quite familiar with the film's concept of an alien coming to earth with a warning that the planet clean up its act or face dire consequences, having seen the original 1951 film several times in his youth. "Science fiction is a genre I enjoy," he told *The Los Angeles Times*. "I guess I'm drawn to these films because there are usually (fun things) in them."

But Keanu remained cautious when approached by the head of 20th Century Fox to play the role of Klaatu, the alien with a message for the world. "I'm not a remake kind of guy. So my question was why," he told *The Los Angeles Times*. "Then I talked to the director Scott Derrickson and I found out that he had the why. I found that he had a real respect for the concept of the original. He thought the story of an alien coming to earth with a warning was a worthwhile tale."

During filming, Keanu walked a fine line, paying homage to actor Michael Rennie's strong, silent portrayal of Klaatu in the original, while adding subtle shades and nuance to his modern take. The film would prove a successful melding of classic science fiction storytelling and modern political and social sensibilities and would do solid, if not spectacular, business in theaters.

Going from a big-budget studio film to an independent low-budget project had pretty much been Keanu's modus operandi for some time. It was a chance to decompress and have a bit of fun away from the inherent pressures of big money Hollywood. But *Henry's Crime* would come with a very big first. After nearly five years of preparation well below the Hollywood radar, Keanu was about to unveil the first effort of his own production company, Company Films. And in conception and execution, *Henry's Crime* would be very much a B movie.

Budgeted at a modest $12 million, *Henry's Crime* is a mixture of romantic comedy and heist film in which the title character, also played by Keanu, plays a less-than-ambitious and gullible working man who ends up doing time in prison for being falsely convicted of a bank robbery. After being released from prison, Henry decides to rob the very bank he was accused of robbing in the first place.

Keanu knew going in that wearing the hats of both producer and the star would be treacherous. "It's somewhat difficult to wear two hats," he admitted to *The Star.* "As an actor, you're supposed to take care of your emotions and, as a producer, you're supposed to take care of other people's emotions."

Henry's Crime ultimately proved to be a

comforting, fairly formulaic bit of fluff, reasonably entertaining and featuring Keanu as a bumbling anti-hero. But even the presence of Keanu and co star James Caan could not keep the film from being released theatrically in only two theaters, and grossing a shade over $8,000 en route to a mere $2.2 million. But the film would ultimately go on to garner a cult following on video.

Street Kings had a bit of a history to it. Early drafts of this police/crime thriller were written by famed crime writer James Ellroy, and the story had, at various points, sparked interest from directors Spike Lee and Oliver Stone. *Street Kings*, a tale of police and political corruption centered around a disillusioned LAPD vice detective, played by Keanu, is sparked by regular and often graphic violence. Given his peace-loving nature, it came as a surprise that Keanu was immediately attracted to the blood and gore surrounding his character.

"I liked the complexity of the character I played," he explained to *Indie London*. "I liked his violence. I was intrigued by the level of violence that seemed to surround him at all times."

Street Kings proved only a moderate success and reviews ran to the high side of mixed. But Keanu looked upon the experience as a winner, in which he was able to play a role that ran contrary to type.

And playing contrary to type was becoming more and more the reason for taking roles at for Keanu. Because, in terms of career choices, he was constantly looking for that creative jolt, the juice that was making an already established career exciting and new.

To the degree that Keanu was willing to fly in the

face of conventional Hollywood thinking during this period was best personified by his running head first into what many consider his most unorthodox film, *Generation Um...* , a film so independent minded in concept and execution as to defy any semblance of logic by even the most liberal-leaning observers.

Generation Um..., the second film produced by his Company Pictures, tells the story of an aimless New York bottom-dweller who makes a living by driving two party girls on their appointed rounds. Seemingly aimless and often meandering in its telling, at the hands of a first-time director, *Generation Um...* is so tightly scripted to the point where moments of sheer improvisation appear to be well thought out. Keanu, who saw much more than youthful angst in the project and its attendant themes of anti-technology and sociology, knew going in that the film would be an uphill battle, especially when it came to critical perceptions.

He was smart enough to realize that his name anywhere on the film would draw a modicum of attention. And to some degree, he was prepared for the critical beating it took. To a person, critics slammed the film as a mindless example of the concept of "mumble-core" and took thinly veiled shots at Keanu for what they perceived as bad acting. *Generation Um...* played in a handful of theaters for what seemed like a microsecond before graduating to "cult status" and finding "guilty pleasure" popularity on the internet circuit.

Generation Um... would be the conclusion of a period where Keanu had dared to be different. What would follow would be more of the same.

CHAPTER TWENTY-FOUR
SAD KEANU AND
THE ODE TO HAPPINESS

Is Keanu lonely? Is Keanu reclusive? Or is he just a normal guy who enjoys his own company and is often spotted doing… well… normal things by himself.

See Keanu shopping. See Keanu going to a bookstore. See Keanu going outside to pick up the newspaper off his front porch. There are countless websites dedicated to Keanu doing absolutely nothing out of the ordinary and, just as often, in the company of nobody.

But this being Keanu, there's always been an undercurrent of evidence that would indicate that, yes, he is truly a lonely guy. A dysfunctional upbringing. The death of a child and the love of his life. The lack of anything approaching a serious relationship for seemingly forever. That would drive any marginal human being into a shell. On a superficial Hollywood level, Keanu is always kind of around, but never for very long. He's soon back into his private world.

Does that equate loneliness? A lot of people seem to think so. But Keanu would beg to differ, as he explained in a conversation with *CoverMedia.com*. "I know a lot of people might not want to believe it for whatever reason but I'm really a happy guy."

That being said, a large percentage of Keanu's fan base continued to bask in the fantasy that their idol and/or dream lover was truly a lonely sad man. That perception would reach its apex in May 2010 when paparazzo Ron Asadorian happened upon the actor sitting alone on a bench, hunched over and looking down in the dumps as he contemplated a sandwich. The photo would eventually go viral courtesy of entertainment syndicate Splash News and would ignite an internet wildfire titled "Sad Keanu" that quickly made its way around the world.

People were flooding media and internet outlets, expressing deep and heartfelt concern about Keanu's emotional and mental state. The whole Sad Keanu phenomena quickly reached a point where Keanu's management was moved to make a public statement on the situation, which was picked up by countless media outlets, including *ABC News*. "Keanu Reeves would like to thank all of his fans for their concerns regarding his happiness and wants to assure you that all is well."

The internet was not ready to let go, however, and the whole Sad Keanu movement would soon turn lighthearted. On June 15, 2010, an international Cheer Up Keanu Reeves Day was declared. Through October, good-natured spoofs by way of doctored Photoshop versions of the original photo would have Sad Keanu sitting next to kittens, inserted into scenes from the movies *Pulp Fiction* and *The Breakfast Club,* and even into a bit of Banksy graffiti art. Keanu finally got wind of what was going on and, in conversation with *Vulture.com*, took it the right way.

"It all sounds like good, clean fun. Do I wish I didn't get my picture taken while I was eating a sandwich in New York? Yeah."

Well before Sad Keanu was trending, Keanu was already having a bit of good-natured fun with the lonely concept when he and artist friend Alexandra Grant cobbled together a slim, jokey, mocking book called *Ode to Happiness*. But before *Ode to Happiness* became a reality, Keanu recalled in separate interviews with *BBC News* and *The Guardian* that it all began as a hoot at a party.

"I was in my kitchen, hanging out with my friend Janey Bergam and the radio was on and this station was playing nostalgic music. This station was playing like an orgy of depressing, self- pitying music. It was so voluptuously horrible and I just started to write on this piece of paper because I had this image of the moment when you take that bath, you light that candle and you're really just kind of depressed. I just kept piling on the self-pity and it was making Janey laugh so hard."

A sampling of what had Keanu's friend doubled over in laughter? "I draw a hot sorrow bath/In my despair room/I wash my hair with regret shampoo/I hate myself face cream/Alone again silk pajamas."

Sometime after Keanu's words had brought his friend to tears, Janey was at a birthday party whose guests included Los Angeles artist Grant. The pair got to talking, and amid renewed laughter, hatched a plan to create a one-off book incorporating Keanu's words and Grant's art, and present it to Keanu as a surprise gift. Grant would take six months and a lot of creative effort to bring Keanu's lighthearted, self-directed jabs to life. "It needed images to match the power of the

137

humor of each line, but also the sadness," Grant recalled. "I wanted to come up with something that matched the DNA of the poem," she recalled to *BBCNews.com* and *The Guardian*.

The finished book was given to Keanu. Grant remembered the moment. "We presented the book to Keanu. It was a surprise. A private gift. We didn't make the book to publish it. But then someone said 'I want five copies' and that's when the lightbulb went on."

And although he saw that initial concept of *Ode to Happiness* as a good-natured and, by him, fun poke at his low-key sense of humor, Keanu also saw some commercial potential in it. "I thought it was fantastic. Holding it, I just had this moment of looking at and going 'wow!' If I'd like to have this, then other people would like to have this."

Keanu and Alexandra took the step of contacting German art book publisher Gerhard Steidl, who immediately agreed to put out *Ode to Happiness* as a limited-edition run of 4000 copies at a collectible price of $50. More of a pop culture art oddity than anything approaching a mainstream celebrity tie-in, *Ode to Happiness* did do quite well in the world of fandom and art, with all copies reportedly selling out in record time and prices approaching four figures on the secondary/rare book market. In any case, Keanu felt that the book had made its point to his satisfaction.

"It's only personal in the sense of looking out and regarding my sense of humor. It is not a reflection of my personal life nor was it designed to counteract my media created lonely image. There's a kind of life experience in it. I was hoping that people would find it relatable and transformative."

In the wake of *Ode to Happiness*, Keanu would often speculate on scratching his newfound writing itch. He admitted to being a bit gun shy at the prospect of writing a novel, and confessed to finding creative comfort in poetry. To the extent that, when talking to *The Guardian*, he speculated that a follow-up book might well be called *Haikus of Hope*, the premise of which was very much in his metaphysical mindset.

"Basically, I want to kill myself and go from there," he teased of the approach the book would take. "Going into such a dark place that you can somehow find the light at the end of the tunnel. But a nice end of the tunnel. Not the end of the tunnel."

CHAPTER TWENTY-FIVE
KEANU'S WAY

Keanu turned 40 in 2005. Forty can be rough on many people. Keanu would be no exception, as he offered in an interview with *Vogue Spain*. "Turning 40 was shocking. I had the sensation of coming to the end of the road that I dreamed as a child. The hopes, dreams and sorrows had either come true or not and that road was over."

Keanu would survive the seeming inner futility of it all. But three years later, it all came rushing back.

Keanu turned 43 in 2008. For real people with real lives, it has become almost a cliché, a time to take stock, a time for new adventures, a time to make up for lost time. But, for Keanu, having spent an entire life in the spotlight, growing old by Hollywood/celebrity standards, and dodging tags like "the ageless wonder" and "Hollywood vampire," the celeb that never seems to age, dealing with the age question can elicit everything from a straightforward "My decision was also tied to getting older," which he told *Reuters* of a decision to take the jump into directing, to a downright Shakespearian response when the age question was posed by *Esquire UK*.

"I'm every cliché. Fucking mortality. Ageing. I'm

just starting to get better at it. Just the amount of stuff you have to do before you're dead. It's all the clichés and it's embarrassing. It's all of them. It's just 'Oh my God! Okay, where did the time go? How come things are changing? How much time do I have left? What didn't I do?' So yeah, I'm that guy."

Getting older on a broad Hollywood stage has continued apace, and Keanu, in conversation with *Mr-Reeves.com*, easily admitted that he'd noticed the changes. "The transition is definitely noticeable. I've suddenly realized that I'm not as flexible as I used to be. Previously, I have not paid too much attention to time. Suddenly I've noticed it. It's like 'where did the last five years go?'"

Whether he wanted to admit it, by 2008, Keanu had emerged as a Hollywood commodity, something of a two-edged sword, if you will. He was talented, bankable and an ideal fit for certain things. It was a status that most actors would kill for. But Keanu was suddenly feeling uneasy with that crown. Yes, the scripts were there for the picking. However nothing was feeling exciting or intriguing. It was starting to feel like he was punching a clock, and Keanu did not like that feeling.

And so, while most would be looking for that easy ride through middle age, Keanu, through the mid-to-late 2000's, was taking chances guided more by intellect and desire than big bucks and the bottom line.

Easily the most cerebral and obscure effort during this period was the documentary *Side by Side*, a detailed look at the rise of classic film and the new kid on the cinematic block, digital. Produced by Keanu and his production company, Company Pictures, *Side By Side*, through interviews with countless filmmakers, answers the questions of how the two formats evolved, the differences between film and digital, and the future of both formats.

Keanu and *Side By Side* director Chris Kenneally had worked together on *Henry's Crime* and had talked at length about the technical side of filmmaking. The idea struck a serious/curious streak in Keanu. "At one point, I asked Chris if he wanted to make a documentary about this," Keanu told *Comingsoon.net*, "and he said yes."

Side By Side was filmed on and off for a period of a year, with the actor having to step aside to complete other film roles. But he would always return to *Side By Side* with a renewed energy that saw him doing a lot of the actual interviews. "The project was very personal to me," he offered *Comingsoon.net*. "I wanted to be part of it. I wanted to get the answers. The questions I asked were my questions."

47 Ronin would take Keanu back to the kind of expensive, big-budget special effects film he had not been involved in since the end of *The Matrix* trilogy. The film, whose story line focuses on the exploits of 18th century Japanese Samurai who run the gauntlet of honor, revenge and impossible love, was shaping up as an extravaganza of international proportions. It included several 3-D sequences, lots of swordplay and a primarily Japanese cast. The initial budget was a reported $175 million. To copper their investment, Universal Studios needed a North American actor who would travel well with a worldwide audience.

Enter Keanu, who, on the surface, seemed a logical choice. Keanu had long been someone who appreciated Asian philosophy, history and religion, and was a devotee of the attitudes they espoused. That he was more than capable of being believable with ancient weaponry was a plus. All that being said, Keanu was not being courted to be "the star" of *47 Ronin* but rather *a* star in what was shaping up as an ensemble cast. But Keanu was intrigued, especially once he read the script.

"When I first read the script, it had the largesse of a Western," he explained to *Screenrant.com*. "The character I played is an outsider seeking to belong. It's a story of drama and revenge. For drama that's good. It sucks in real life."

47 Ronin would provide a number of challenges, many of which were technological and international concerns. Keanu would go back to school on a couple of fronts. The actor would spend months learning the intricacies of swordplay and would take a crash course in Japanese. He ended up shooting much of his dialogue scenes in both English and Japanese. The 3-D elements of the film would necessitate endless takes and subtle movement changes to accommodate the 3-D movements.

In conversations with *The Los Angeles Times* and *Associated Press* during the making of the film, Keanu was effusive in saying that he felt *47 Ronin* was something special. "We're trying to make a movie with a lot of depth and in more ways than one. The film tells of people who share this journey to reclaim their land, their honor and their way of life. It was very special for me to be a part of it."

Unfortunately, what had started out as a potentially great experience soon found *47 Ronin* going off the rails. According to reports in the likes of *TheWrap.com, The Guardian* and *Screenrant.com*, early reports from the set and the first rough cut of the film were not encouraging. Owing to the director Carl Rinsch's vision and his reported inability to gain control of what had turned into a massive filmmaking process, Universal was not happy with what they were seeing.

A big problem was that Keanu's character was seemingly marginalized away from center stage for much of the film, and for an actor with that kind of box office clout, he was largely invisible. Universal stepped in and demanded a week's worth of reshoots in an attempt to put more Keanu on film. The reshoots included the addition of a Keanu love scene, a number of closeups of Keanu in pivotal moments in the film, additional dialogue scenes and an increased presence in the film's climactic battle sequence. Still not satisfied after the reshoots, Universal essentially took the film away from the director and edited the picture's final cut themselves.

This resulted in the film's budget ballooning to $225 million and several delays in *47 Ronin's* release date, amid dire media predictions that the film would be a money loser of massive proportions. The film would finally open in Japan to disappointing box office and paved the way for an onslaught of bad reviews. Despite grossing an estimated $151 million, *47 Ronin* would go down in flames as a bomb, a money loser and a black mark on Keanu's career.

To the end, Keanu would remain a staunch defender of *47 Ronin*, often citing the inherent ambition and execution of what many would consider a flawed film. But it was safe to say that by the time *47 Ronin* hit theaters, Keanu was already preoccupied with something else. In fact, years before *47 Ronin*, Keanu had been laying the groundwork for his directorial debut, the very

Hong Kong-style action epic, *The Man of Tai Chi*. It was a film whose origin went back to his *The Matrix* days and his fight trainer on all three films, Tiger Chen.

Post *Matrix*, Keanu and Tiger remained in touch and would become good friends. "Tiger was starting to act," Keanu related to *Vulture.com*. "We decided we wanted to work together and we started developing a story."

The development of *The Man of Tai Chi* would evolve over a number of years, beginning in 2007, into a tale of a purist martial arts fighter (Tiger) who needs to make money and soon finds himself fighting in professional underground fights, overseen by a crime boss named Donaka Mark. Tiger soon finds himself tempted by the material perks of the professional fight game and ultimately must fight for redemption and his purist soul. As envisioned by Keanu, the film would be very much in the tradition of such Hong Kong classics as *Five Fingers of Death* and its U.S. counterpart *Enter the Dragon*, with a sprinkling of *A Most Dangerous Game*, and a literal buffet of dialogue shot in English, Mandarin and Cantonese language.

Over a period of five years, Keanu and Tiger worked developing the script and getting funding from primarily foreign investment organizations. During this time, Keanu and Tiger worked closely and, for Keanu, obsession was just around the corner. "It became so much of my heart and mind," he told *Vulture.com*. "It was a story I wanted to tell. It was a story I wanted to direct."

Keanu danced around approaching Tiger with the idea of his making his directorial debut on *The Man of Tai Chi*. He knew it would be a large commitment on Tiger's part to put a film that was pivotal in his career with somebody with no professional directing experience, a situation that could possibly ruin their friendship. The question was finally broached, as Keanu recalled to *Indiewire.com*. "I asked Tiger if it was okay if I directed the film and he immediately said yes. I said thank you."

When Keanu was announced as the film's director, the already significant buzz went into overdrive. First-time directors had not always had the best luck on their maiden voyage and Keanu, for all his positive attitude and significant insights into martial arts filmmaking, making *The Man of Tai Chi* would certainly be a trial by fire. Especially when it was decided that Keanu, besides directing, would also play the role of the crime overlord Donaka Mark.

But Keanu was confident that he knew what the film, in his hands, would be about. "I wanted to have fun with it," he explained to *Vulture.com*. "I felt like the film should be bigger than life and have no rules." He was going in well prepared in dealing with both the expected fight scenes and the character moments. And by this time, Keanu was well versed in the dollars and cents of the movie business, and the people who would be less than subtle if he were to lose control of the film. "The toughest hurdle was just time and money," he offered to *The Daily Beast*. "Sometimes your hopes and dreams don't match up with the budget and you have to get creative and use your imagination to get things done."

Keanu did not wander onto the set of *Man of Tai Chi* a babe in the woods. In previous outings he had been conspicuous by his attention to details; things like camera angles and the placement of actors in a particular shot. Producing *Henry's Crime* and *Side By Side* gave him an up-close-and personal look at the

147

business side of movies. Consequently, he exuded confidence and poise in his first directing opportunity.

"I didn't feel like I had to make a phone call to anybody asking 'What do I do?'" he told the *New York Times*. "I felt like I could see the forest and the trees."

Among the primarily Asian actors that populated the cast, Keanu would prove to be a subtle taskmaster who earned their respect with his drive to do more than was necessary. Tiger recalled how Keanu drove him, saying in conversation with the *New York Times*, "Keanu wanted me to go over the top with my energy in every take. If I went 100 percent that wasn't enough. I had to go 120 percent."

However, Tiger would get a bit of payback when it was time for Keanu, as the villainous Donaka Mark, to go toe to toe in a pivotal fight sequence. Keanu would be the first to admit that his combat skills had grown rusty with age and, when coupled with the element of having to direct himself in a fight sequence against the man who had taught him just about everything he know about martial arts, people on the set during the fight were holding their collective breath.

Tiger would be diplomatic in assessing Keanu's skills in conversation with *Vulture.com*. "He (Keanu) tried so hard. He hurt himself many, many times. But he was not holding back. We both hit each other pretty hard."

As filming progressed, the ongoing concern would be the question of how Keanu the director would handle Keanu the actor. Keanu joked to*Vulture.com* "Directing myself? It was okay. Reeves came prepared. He was able to hit his mark and he knew his lines."

CHAPTER TWENTY-SIX
KEANU AND ALEXANDRA
GET THAT WAY

While the first inkling that Keanu Reeves and Alexandra Grant were serious business came in November 2019 when they were spotted holding hands on the red carpet of a LACMA art party, the reality was that Keanu and Alexandra had known each other for at least 10 years.

They tended to travel in the same social circles, the art/literature/Hollywood crowd and were often on the same VIP guest lists. Alexandra was a well-respected, accomplished artist with an international reputation and whose impressionistic/hyper-reality works had hung in countless galleries. She was tall with prematurely gray hair and chiseled features that, when combined with an intellectual/artsy way of carrying herself, displayed a sense of low-key elegance and style. Then there was Keanu who, at most parties, was easy to talk to, but often quietly in the background and introspective.

Consequently, it was not surprising that at a 2010 dinner party Keanu, then 45, and Alexandra, 36, were introduced and began a light and easy conversation. There was a shorthand between them during that early exchange. They liked the same artists, literature and movies. Their philosophical and societal attitudes were in synch. They smiled and laughed easily. By the end of the night, they had become fast friends. In a dual interview with Keanu and Alexandra in *Vogue* Spain, there was joking banter from the pair about that first meeting.

Keanu: "When did we first meet Alexandra? Was it in 2010?"

Alexandra: "Yes, that's when it was."

Keanu: "Yes, we met on a friend's birthday."

Alexandra: "We cooked some awesome steaks."

Keanu: "The steaks were really good. And we really became friends as we talked."

Alexandra: "So that party was our first celebration."

Keanu: "Our first anniversary."

That first anniversary resulted in the gag gift turned serious publishing venture *Ode to Happiness*. At this point they seemed like good friends and that any time they were spotted together it was probably 'just business' or simply friends hanging out. They were often off in different parts of the world, working on individual projects, but they were constantly in touch, and good-natured banter was often their touchstone. They were bohemian in a spontaneous sense and that attitude would spur their next collaboration in 2013.

Keanu was in Los Angeles, beginning work on *John Wick,* while Alexandra was in Paris discussing various projects when she was approached by a former *Playboy* magazine editor and, as explained by Alexandra in the publications *Big Life Magazine* and *Vogue* Spain, she recalled: "The editor asked me if Keanu and I could get together again and create a new text image for *Zeitgeist Magazine*. Since we had worked together before on *Ode to Happiness*, it seemed like a natural collaboration that *Zeitgeist* would want my photography and Keanu's poetry. Despite the late hour, Alexandra immediately sent Keanu an invitation to do the project, quoting Malcolm Lowry's classic poem *Under the Volcano*, whose lines read 'I have no house. Only a shadow. But whenever you are in need of a shadow my shadow is yours.'"

For Keanu, the missive was more than a bit seductive and suggestive, a very artsy, meaningful move on Alexandra's part. How Keanu took it was anybody's guess but he would admit to *Vogue* Spain that he "was really inspired."

Keanu's thoughts raced to notions of mourning and mortality and he set to work jotting down lines that he almost immediately sent back to Alexandra. The stanza of verse that immediately caught Alexandra's eye was. "I was born twisted. I do not want to die." Alexandra was immediately jolted out an early morning haze by what she read. "It was very intense," she reflected in *Vogue* Spain. "I needed to make coffee when I received it."

The *Zeitgeist* assignment ultimately fell through, but by that time, the concept of what would finally be put out by the same publisher who published *Ode to Happiness* as *Shadows* had already taken hold in Keanu and Alexandra's minds. "What struck me about the idea of *Shadows* was the play between interior and exterior," he reflected in *Big Life Magazine*. "*Shadows* are evocative, provocative to me. And I liked the idea of writing in short form."

With a book deal for *Shadows* in place, Keanu and Alexandra had their first photo shoot for the project in early November, 2013 in New York. While technical in its conception, the session seemed to indicate the first moments of intimacy and trust between the two artists. So much so that when interviewed by *Vogue* Spain, the pair seemed to throw aside their attitudes toward keeping their private moments private and gleefully talked deeply about that first session.

"The concept was to have a light source in the middle of the darkness," recalled Alexandra. "So I went to your apartment in the afternoon, moved the furniture and took the photos." Keanu picked up the odyssey. "I took off my shoes, took off my jeans and then we started."

Throughout the first and subsequent sessions, Keanu was an amenable, willing puppet to Alexandra's requests. Light and shadow played out as Keanu danced, emphasized body parts in pensive poses and basically threw himself into what Alexandra was asking for. "I remember you mocking me for how I was directing you," she laughingly jogged Keanu's memory. "I didn't tell you to move left or right or to move your arm."

Keanu continued the interview back and forth. "It was a question of 'show me your vulnerability,' 'show me the loneliness. As an actor you need a clear vision. I revoked that for you. That's how the instrument comes to life. You're playing it and I provide the music."

Alexandra ended their artistic journey quite simply when she offered, "I have to say that it was an honor to do that."

Intimacy on an artistic level was a success. It appeared that the rest would follow in due time. But it would be carried out in such a low-key, below-the-radar fashion as to confound even the most intense gossip columnists and paparazzi. What were business moments and what were the first signs of a budding romance were maddeningly inconsistent.

TheCheatsheet.com reported that the couple had been seen together as early as 2013, the most breathless report citing an intimate Thanksgiving dinner at an out-of-the way restaurant. *Entertainment Tonight* reported that things between the pair most certainly began to heat up around 2016 when they spotted on the red carpet of an art gala in Basel, Switzerland.

The consensus eventually was that Keanu and Alexandra were romantically involved by 2017. This was the year they joined creative forces in starting up the publishing firm, *X Artists Books,* and were often spotted together at book-related events. Jennifer Tilly related to the *New York Post* an up-close-and personal view of the budding romance at an art opening for Alexandra's work. "I saw them together at her last art opening and he was not wanting the spotlight at all. He was really a low-key guy which, if you know anything about Alexandra at all, you know she's very low key herself. In that sense, they are perfectly matched."

And not willing to go into seclusion to protect their secrets. Between 2017 and 2019 they were often spotted together at restaurants and just being out together, in a sly sense almost daring the outside world to make something out of what may or may not have been reality. However, a 2016 interview with Keanu and Alexandra found the pair in a teasing mood as they talked philosophy and art with Vogue Spain.

"We are all the same," said Alexandra. "We are people who eat. We are people who want to be loved. The most beautiful thing is the ability to see the divine in another person." Keanu likewise reflected on the universality and infinite personal possibilities when he offered, "You cannot set limits. The clothes we wear, the things we create. These are living things. Real things."

By 2019, the cat was literally out of the bag in June when the pair was spotted together at the Saint Laurent's men's fashion show. To onlookers there was no doubt that, even though their official coming out as a couple would not be until November, the world at large was now seemingly unshakeable in their belief that...

Keanu and Alexandra were a couple and that they were very much in love.

CHAPTER TWENTY-SEVEN
KEANU KILLS THEM ALL

Keanu was on a bit of a decline by 2014. Everything he had attempted over the previous three years, whether by choice or the luck of the draw, had observers of the film scene scratching their heads.

Why an actor who was at the top of his game and in demand for projects by some of the biggest studios would deliberately do a series of projects that were destined for obscurity and, even worse, commercial failure, was beyond them. Bottom line, nothing he had done since *The Matrix* series had been less than entertaining and, on various levels, interesting. But they came and went in the blink of an eye and barely registered in filmgoer's consciousness.

Quite simply, Keanu was suddenly, in the eyes of many Hollywood observers, the equivalent of a marginal baseball player. Good field no hit. In recent years, Keanu's eclectic choices have become the topic du jour with many entertainment journalists, and Keanu has been patient in responding, acknowledging a propensity for changing things up and doing smaller projects with up-and-coming filmmakers. "Although I haven't made any big Hollywood productions in recent years, with the exception of *47 Ronin*, I have been working pretty regularly. I don't think in terms of making a great comeback."

But Keanu would finally be succinct on the subject as a quote from *Popsugar.com* makes clear: "I finally just said fuck the bucks. I decided to go for the experience in the things I was choosing."

It was at that moment that *John Wick* brought about just such an experience. On the surface, *John Wick* appeared to be pretty simple action stuff. A bunch of Russia mob toughs steal Wick's car and kill his dog. What they fail to realize was that John Wick is one of the world's greatest assassins, psychologically damaged by the recent death of his wife and now pushed over the edge with the murder of his dog. Wick is out for revenge and proves unstoppable as he metes out bloody and violent revenge on seemingly the entire population of New York. Keanu was immediately attracted to the big-budget, robust action and violence, and was keen to play the stoic loner out for revenge. But he also saw the role as something much deeper than the obvious.

Although he only hinted at it in interviews, he saw much of himself in a character struck by tragedy. "For the character and in life, it's about the love of the person you're grieving for and anytime you can keep company with that fire, it's warm," he waxed philosophically to *The Guardian*. "I absolutely relate to that and I don't think you ever work through it."

But he stopped short of saying that he would exact revenge because of it and that, in real life, he did not own a gun, but did concede that he got a certain adrenaline rush when holding a weapon in his hand. He admitted that the *John Wick* storyline was made of more biblical stuff when questioned by the *GMA*

Network. "It's kind of an Old Testament story. When someone takes the things he cherishes, violence erupts and he just can't challenge it."

During a round of interviews in Korea in which Keanu answered questions from the likes of *The Korea Times* and *The Korea Herald*, and delved deeper into the character who, to his way of thinking, was more than a mere conduit for violence and revenge. "John Wick is a hero unto himself. It's not only about revenge. He's fighting for his inner life, the grief and love he feels about the loss of his wife. He's both the hero and the antihero. I love how he suffers. I love his passion and his will."

There was a lot riding on *John Wick*, both said and unsaid, as Keanu went before the cameras. On paper, the film seemed to have smash hit written all over it and, by association, it would position Keanu to potentially front a tent pole action franchise that could finally put him in the pantheon of such elder statesmen of the action genre as Bruce Willis, Sylvester Stallone and Arnold Schwarzenegger. But Keanu knew that, despite being in his 50's, he would need to come across as believable as an aging super-assassin out for blood. Consequently, he would train long and hard and was quite specific in learning exactly what each action sequence would require. He admitted that he was physically working harder than ever and that he was, by degrees, also slowing down. He insisted, often times to the filmmaker's chagrin, that he would do most of his own stunts, fights, and driving gags.

The degree to which Keanu would literally put his life on the line was much in evidence during the filming of a pivotal and prolonged violent sequence in a New York nightclub. The night of the scheduled shoot, Keanu had reportedly come down with the flu and was running a temperature of 104 degrees. He was extremely sick and should have been in bed. But Keanu insisted that he could do the scene and, as the director and the rest of the cast and crew watched with bated breath, Keanu fought through an all-night shoot that included running, jumping, gunplay, and bloody fights. Everybody watched for the first sign of trouble. But Keanu, fighting the illness and mustering up the will, much like the character he was playing, made it through the last shot of the night.

John Wick would be the touchstone that Keanu was looking for. It would open to rave reviews and box office on an international scale. By the end of its first week in theaters, there was already talk of a sequel or sequels. Keanu had a franchise he could call his own.

Now that he was back in the rarified air of Hollywood success (had he ever really left?), Keanu slipped back into below-the-radar projects. The first was a low-budget, made-in-Chile horror shocker called *Knock, Knock*. Directed and written by torture porn pioneer Eli Roth, *Knock Knock* follows a man left alone by his family on Father's Day. He answers a knock on the door and is face to face with two young girls looking for a party. The man succumbs to their sexual advances and what follows is a psychosexual game that turns bloody and violent en route to a grim, downbeat ending. Keanu, just off a big-budget movie in which he was the hero, going into something like *Knock, Knock* was a massive change of pace. Keanu had always been an admirer of Roth's, and responded to the offer in an attempt to wind down from the rigors of *John Wick*, largely for the opportunity the film gave him to be the victim rather than another hero.

The year 2016 was easily one of the busiest times of Keanu's career. He would appear in five different films, largely of a small independent nature, in various roles, one could question whether Keanu was an undiscriminating workaholic or his moves were an attempt to keep his mind fresh with a series of films that would barely see the light of day. *Exposed* was a pretty much by-the-numbers police crime thriller that came and went in with little fanfare.

For the buddy cop action comedy *Keanu,* Keanu the actor was literally a cameo, voicing the voice of a cat named Keanu. Keanu had a miniscule role as Hank the lecherous motel owner in the psychologically and critically offensive horror film *The Neon Demon*. Easily Keanu's strangest choice during this period was the role of a cult leader in a dystopian future in the film *The Bad Patch*, a grade-C thriller with cannibalism, blood, violence, and gunplay, all set against a nihilistic desert backdrop.

Another movie that had some moments but was gone in a flash and had a very limited theatrical release was *The Whole Truth*. Perhaps actor Daniel Craig knew something nobody else did, because a mere three days before *The Whole Truth* was set to begin filming, he unexpectedly dropped out of the movie. Consequently, Keanu, in a rare situation in which he was a back-up choice, took over the role of a crusading defense lawyer caught up in legal rights and wrongs. Like everything else Keanu did in 2016, *The Whole Truth* was, for all intents and purposes, a straight-to-cable entry with a microscopic theatrical appearance.

Theories were floated as to why Keanu voluntarily allowed himself what was, generously, a mediocre string of films. Some ventured that the actor had somehow lost all his money and was doing anything to pay the bills. But Keanu, ever the diplomat, waxed positive on these questionable choices when he talked to *Collider.com*.

"I guess I've just had these opportunities recently. There's just been some interesting roles and interesting material."

CHAPTER TWENTY-EIGHT
IS KEANU A VAMPIRE?

Is Keanu a vampire?

Although there have never been reports of his sucking blood or flitting about at night on little bat wings, there is a sizeable segment of fandom, admittedly a part of the fanatic/lunatic fringe, that is convinced that Keanu is truly some kind of immortal. And, depending on how far one wants to stretch the bonds of reality and fantasy, there is fragmentary evidence that would suggest that the actor has already lived long and prospered.

By 2019, two of Keanu's seminal works, *Bill & Ted's Excellent Adventure* and *The Matrix,* were celebrating the 30th and 25th anniversaries of their original releases. Those into speculation are quick to point out that Keanu in photos from that period are shockingly similar to how Keanu, at age 55, looks in 2020. Adding campy fuel to the fire is a popular fringe website called *Keanu Is Immortal,* which has gone to great lengths to make a case for Keanu actually having been around since the 1500's and, in particular, pointing to the similarities between Keanu and such historical figures as Charlemagne and Paul Monet.

Keanu had heard all these rumors of vampirism

and immortality for years, and, during an appearance on *The Tonight Show with Jimmy Fallon*, he chose, with tongue firmly planted in cheek, to address them.

"We're all stardust baby," he cracked to Fallon before agreeing that there were some similarities between himself and Monet. "I can see we have a likeness in the eyes, the nose, the moustache, the beard and the cheekbones and the forehead."

To the degree that Keanu seemed to be poking good natured fun at the "Keanu is a vampire" theory was very plain in a conversation that appeared in *Tentstile.com*, when he laughingly reported that he was not using face cream designed to delay the aging process but, just as quickly added fuel to the fire when he said that his seeming lack of aging "might have something to do with my ancestors."

But vampire aside, Keanu does seem to have found a lifestyle that keeps him looking young. He has often admitted to having a positive outlook on life that includes quiet time, often with a good book, good music, good art, and that he does not tend to occupy his mind with negative thoughts. Physically, he leads a healthy lifestyle, and while he is mum on specifics, he apparently has no magic diet but, rather eats several healthy balanced meals per day. He works out regularly, basketball and weightlifting being two favorite forms of exercise, even when not preparing for a film role.

"I've had a personal trainer for 10 years," Keanu told *Grazia*, "and if she doesn't hear from me for too long, she brings me back on track."

Keanu is aware and in awe of the passage of time. As he offered to *BrainyQuote.com*, "How do I confront aging? With a sense of wonder and a sense of terror." In *Esquire* UK he addressed the public interest. "People just keep saying my age and I'm just waiting for that to change."

However Keanu chooses to quantify the age issue, one thing is certain. He has little time or use to contemplate the age-old question of what might have been, a thought that tends to dog everybody at a certain point. "I don't think about lost youth," he said in an interview with *MrReeves.com*. "That only occurs to people who feel they have not lived their lives. That does not apply to me."

CHAPTER TWENTY-NINE
KEANU: OLDER AND WISER

Keanu was well into his 50's by 2017.

Always somebody who was self-assured and confident in his own rebellious way, the actor, with stardom and worldwide celebrity well in hand, would seem relaxed and poised with, if we're being honest, no new worlds to conquer. He could do what he wanted, when he wanted, and get rewarded quite handsomely for it. In every sense of the word, Keanu had made it. But security would make him anything but complacent.

"It (acting) is a hustle," Keanu told *Arizona Central.com*, then "We're all beggars in this business. I can't do this alone. You get offers and if the film isn't for you, then you can say 'no thank you'. If the movie is for you then you definitely have to work at it."

And no matter what he says yes to, Keanu, even at the advanced stages of his career, is still the perfectionist and still has moments of fear. "I worry that people won't like what I do," he offered to *Women's Health*. "I'm telling stories, that's what it's about for me. I just hope that people will like the stories I'm telling." And Keanu is adamant that even the action films that he has become famous for have to have some legitimate rhyme and reason to get him interested. "I love action films," he told *The Belfast Telegraph.* "But they have to have a story and a real filmmaker behind them. I don't want to just start doing them just for the sake of showing up and collecting a paycheck."

Keanu did not have to wait long for his action film checklist to be filled' literally as the first film was hitting theaters, a script was already being hammered out for what would be *John Wick: Chapter 2*, a film that picks up where the first film ended, as everybody's favorite super-assassin once again attempts to retire from the life only to be informed that the Russian mob has put out an open contract on him. Reluctantly, Wick digs his heavy arsenal out of its tomb and is again on the blood-soaked road of extreme violence and his own brand of justice.

As befitting the international smash hit that *John Wick, John Wick Chapter 2* was outfitted with twice the budget, much of which went toward amped-up violence and action. Keanu acknowledged as much when talking to *Esquire*, saying, "I think a lot of people's response to the first film was that once you kill a dog, you can do just about whatever you want." But he was just as adamant that *Chapter 2* would not just be more of the same, when he offered in *Reuters* and *Associated Press* that the world was expanding. "I like the depth of John's feeling. I like how he fights for his life. We had great ideas with this one. We've opened up the world."

Keanu was in a "right frame of mind" as he contemplated readying himself for what would be a massive amount of preparation. As befitting a big-budget, schedule-conscious sequel, the prolonged fight sequences and all manner of action would be synched to the moment, with seemingly little room for on- set improvisation. Keanu was willingly up for what followed, a three-month intensive training period in which he would get down and dirty with martial arts movements, what is called in the trade gun work, fight choreography, and stunt driving. "I love all the training," Keanu enthused to the *Associated Press*.

As usual, there was the occasional tug of war between Keanu's desire to do all his own stunts and the production's bottom-line desire to not kill their star in the middle of filming. Keanu would insist that he could do everything, which was a constant source of amusement and admiration to those around him, and, more often than not, the director would relent and give the star a shot. Keanu would prove particularly adept at handling the wheel of his '69 Mustang in a literal bang-up of a car action sequence in which, under the hopeful eyes of the filmmakers, he was at the wheel when he rammed his car into another vehicle with such ferocity that he sheared off the steering column in his hand.

Keanu told *Associated Press* that when it came to playing with heavy artillery, his preparation "required a lot of homework. I basically just took the gun home with me. I started walking around with it, spying rooms, practicing draws and reloads and transitioning from weapon to weapon. Then it was just a matter of putting it all together in a John Wick style."

John Wick: Chapter 2 was a whole lot of hard work and nobody would have blamed Keanu if he took some time off, especially since the at-large speculation was that *Chapter 2* would be a huge film and that a third film was already in the writing stage. But after a typical short period of R&R, Keanu was once again restless. Which would lead to a particularly rough critical patch.

Keanu decided to co-star with old friend Winona Ryder in *Destination Wedding*, a predictable slice of rom com in which they play polar opposite wedding guests who overcome their differences and live happily ever after. Nothing special here, except this nine-day wonder did allow two friends to get together for old times' sake in a fairly harmless exercise. Things would get a bit choppier with Keanu's dramatic turns in *Siberia* (a diamond dealer thriller in the wilds of Russia) and *Replicas* (in which a scientist attempts to resurrect his dead family to predictably unpredictable results. The latter two films, both co-produced by Keanu's company, would prove conspicuous by their choppy writing, directing and acting, and would be considered sub-B level filmmaking en route to money-losing theatrical releases and a quick exile to cable film sites.

For Keanu, this would be a period of some piling-on in which his integrity, questionable deal-making and alleged downright laziness—aka cash grab—were floated. Keanu did a minimal amount of promotion for *Siberia* and *Replicas* before fading into semi seclusion as he awaited what would shortly be the start of *John Wick 3: Parabellum*.

The *John Wick* franchise had almost instantly arrived as a movie industry perennial, a guaranteed hit and a series that could quite easily go on forever. But there was a potential downside to a *Part 3* of even the most powerful film series.

History has proven that even successful franchises can find themselves timid about expanding the concept, instead relying on the tried and true, eventually sliding into predictability and product mentality. One need only look at the totally underappreciated *Hellraiser* series, which followed three very imaginative outings with a gradual slide into formula that would ruin its reputation in five quickie, cable-level fodder sequels that totally lost the potential and creativity.

But Keanu and the by now-stock company of filmmakers, writers and stunt people were not about to cut John Wick off at the knees. And a big part of that was the gentle insistence by Keanu that he have some input into the script. Keanu admitted to wanting certain things. "I love the character and I love the world," Keanu told *Collider.com*. "I haven't been able to contribute much to the story in the first two films as I do with this story. I'm learning how to do that and it's been fun to explore."

And "fun" offered up the opportunity to let Keanu's imagination run wild somewhere there had to be ninjas. He also wanted some John Wick-on-horseback desert action. "I always thought that it would be cool if John Wick escaped on a horse, rode horses and fought while on horseback," he told *Collider.com*. "And why not have him fighting ninjas? I always thought it would be cool if John Wick were wearing a suit while fighting in the desert."

But at the end of the day, all the stunt work would have meant little if the story did not expand the concept of a world of hit men chasing down the super-hitman who had broken the code. Hence a storyline that, while again having John Wick on the run and engaging in numerous bits of high body count violence, went deeper into the conceit and the mentality and hinted at what challenges still remained, as Wick went toe-to-toe with the top-secret group The High Table. "We've got some cool story ideas here that are opening up the world, he told *Collider.com*. For Keanu, much of the preparation for *John Wick 3: Parabellum* was, by now, rote. Lots of specialized training, which included learning to ride a horse; much more stylized if, by degrees, less choreographed gunplay; and assorted blood-letting. By the end of the shoot, *John Wick 3: Parabellum* had successfully morphed into something that was as much art and depth as it was commerce.

And that's exactly what made it something worth doing. And for Keanu, it was the carrot that his run as the baddest man on the planet was not over.

CHAPTER THIRTY
KEANU PLAYS KEANU

Keanu is a very funny guy. Believe it or not.

It all depends on who you talk to. A lot of people who have been up close and personal with the actor swear that behind his self-effacing, low-key personality is a razor-sharp, rapier-like wit who can make party guests double over in laughter with a look or quip. Others tend to line up behind the notion that Keanu could not tell a joke if his life depended on it. And then there are those internet dwellers who live and die by the idea that anything Keanu does in his everyday life is a joke all to itself.

So is Keanu a laugh-a-minute kind of guy? It might be time to go to the source. In typical Keanu fashion, the actor ducked and weaved questions about his sense of humor and, likewise, he managed to squeeze in an aside as to the real Keanu humor in conversation with *Playgirl.*

"I'm weird. I hate seeing pictures of myself where I have this look in my eye that says 'Oh I'm sensitive and deep.' I hate that puppy dog look. I'd rather people see pictures of me being cross eyed and making some stupid face."

In 2019, Keanu would, figuratively, get a chance to

171

make a stupid face in a critically acclaimed cameo in a Netflix romantic comedy called *Always Be My Maybe*. The film, directed by Nahnatchka Khan and starring comedian Ali Wong and actor Randall Park, follows the up-and-down relationship of two former lovers who reunite years later and begin a rollercoaster journey of unrequited feelings and current lifestyles as they decide if and how to rekindle their love. As the script went through early drafts it became evident that the film-makers had Keanu on their mind for a mid-film extended cameo in which Wong introduces her former lover to her current beau, who just happens to be Keanu Reeves.

But not *that* Keanu Reeves. In keeping with the comedy aspect of the film, the filmmakers had fashioned a Keanu literally from the bizarro world, an obnoxious, self-centered, ego-driven Keanu immersed in his own celebrity, whose drive to be the alpha dog in any situation is rife with laughs, making good-natured fun of the real Keanu's perceived persona. This alternative-universe Keanu would only be on screen for two scenes and less than 15 minutes screen time.

But early in the process, while Keanu was at the top of their wish list, the filmmakers knew the odds of landing the actor, especially in a role that pokes unadulterated fun at the real Keanu's public perception, would be a long shot. Add to that was the fact that Keanu was in the middle of shooting *John Wick 3: Parabellum* at the time.

"We all thought it was going to be impossible to get him," Park told *Vulture.com.* "What was the likelihood of his being available and then also him being willing to play himself in such a manner?"

Wong was, likewise, hopeful but skeptical as she

172

explained to *Rolling Stone*. "We thought there was no way we'd get him. The list of actors who are willing to play themselves and make fun of themselves, and then on top of that are funny and that can act, is really small. And Keanu is really kind of elusive."

The filmmakers came up with a list of possible backup actors for the Keanu role, among them *Iron Chef America* chairman Mark Dacascos, director M. Night Shyamalan and actor Paul Giamatti. All these choices seemed to have some potential, but ultimately the talks once again came around to Keanu. So they decided to give it a shot and sent an early draft of the script to his management, who in turn, sent it to Keanu. Keanu had been a long-time fan of Wong's stand-up career, especially her concert film *Baby Cobra*, and as he read the script, he got it.

"It was a lot of fun to play a version of myself in an alternative universe," he told *Vanity Fair*. Keanu asked to meet with Khan and Wong at the Chateau Marmont hotel. Keanu was burning the midnight oil, heavily into training for an upcoming round of *John Wick 3* action, in which he was reportedly hanging from a rope in a warehouse and executing kicks and punches. Consequently, he was somewhat the worse for wear when he walked through the Chateau Marmont lobby, wearing a black leather jacket and a motorcycle helmet. The real life moment would mirror his introductory scene in *Always Be My Maybe,* in which he walks through a crowded restaurant with all eyes on him. Khan would recall that moment in conversation with *Vulture.com.*

"He floated in like a goddamned movie star. I think the entire Chateau just went silent for a moment. There was just this different aura about him. It was wild."

By the time introductions between Keanu and Khan and Wong were made and the trio got down to business, the actor had immediately morphed into what Khan described as "humble, funny and well prepared." Reporting second hand in *Vulture.com*, Khan was effusive in reporting how Keanu complemented Wong. "He told Ali that 'He loved that she was so ballsy. You take no prisoners and I love that. I would be honored to be a part of this love story.'"

Wong was equally impressed. She recalled in *Rolling Stone* that he had read the entire script and was very detail-oriented in discussing the story. "At one point he said 'Well I have a question about page 80. Nahnatchka and I looked at each other. I had looked at that draft so many times that I could not even remember what happened on page 80."

During the meeting, Keanu seemed to have already made up his mind that he wanted to do the film. He was in overdrive, pitching his own ideas to the filmmakers, such as wearing glasses with no lenses in them and, in another scene, suggesting that the sequence might come across as funny if his alter ego Keanu recited the name of Chinese dignitaries. At one point, he suddenly took Wong's hand and held it for an awkwardly long time. "It was unbelievable how much he had already committed to the film at that moment and just how shockingly funny he was," she told *Rolling Stone*.

Shortly after the meeting, Keanu sent word that he would be happy to do the part. Now came the issue of how to fit in what would be a four-day break in the filming of *John Wick 3*. Admittedly, Keanu was dead on his feet at that point and could have used the break to do nothing but sleep. But his enthusiasm for the project had gotten his adrenaline going and he would readily agree to give up rest for *Always Be My Maybe.*

On the day filming began, Keanu's star presence was very much on display as people the filmmakers had never seen before were popping out of nowhere to get a glimpse of the actor as he wandered onto the set. As that first day of filming unfolded, it was soon evident that Keanu was very much up to the task of playing a truly fictional version of himself. Pretension and playing things broad were very much on his mind during his restaurant sequence, playing a pampered, ego-driven and fashion-conscious self that rang bombastic and true on just about every level.

As it turned out, spontaneity and improvisation were very much part of *Always Be My Maybe's* master plan, and Keanu was encouraged to step in if he had a suggestion that might play better than what was on the written page. *Indiewire.com* chronicled one such moment when Keanu was heard to suggest, "I have a couple of alternative jokes if you want to try them." It would turn out that Keanu's suggestions were so good that they ended up in the final cut of the film.

One recurring theme in Keanu's *Always Be My Maybe* turn was his innate ability to both make sense and execute what many consider his most challenging role in many decades and, at the same time, be true to his attitude of team player and doing what was best for the film. This trait was much in evidence during his brief stint on *Always Be My Maybe*, as co-star Wong's raved to *Indiewire.com* "Keanu took great pains to not make his character too cartoony because that would have hurt my character. He was very considerate that way. He was super thoughtful."

While *Always Be My Maybe* was well-thought-out romantic comedy as a whole, the consensus was, as postulated in *Gulf News*, a classic case of screen theft in which Keanu was playing his most challenging role... himself. "Keanu was completely compelling," Khan told *Gulf News*. "He totally got it. He realized how his character fit in. He's not the butt of the joke. He's in on the joke with us."

CHAPTER THIRTY-ONE
KEANU IN THREE'S AND FOUR'S

Keanu rumors were all over the place. He was rumored to be in the running for a part of some substance in the next *Fast and the Furious* film. Marvel was continuing their relentless pursuit of the actor for any part he wanted in the next big comic book extravaganza. But Keanu was far too busy to dabble in speculation. Because into 2019, he was already up to his elbows in sequels.

John Wick 3: Parabellum was in post-production and readying a release that was a slam-dunk for major box office. Keanu had barely washed the blood and violence off his psychic clothing when he was offered a voiceover gig in *Toy Story 4*. *Bill & Ted Face the Music*, a third entry in the series that had been in various stages of pre-production for at least a decade, was finally a go. And just when you thought that Keanu would eventually get some time off for good behavior, it was announced in 2019 that *Matrix 4* was truly a go and that Neo would fight once more.

With this rush of A-level projects, observers of Keanu's life and career were all over themselves in proclaiming that the actor had entered a true golden age of prosperity, a Keanussance if you will, and that a lifetime of hard and varied work had finally brought him to the brink of greatness and a revival of immense stature.

Keanu's response to these newfound accolades was typical, self-effacing and "@ho me? A revival?" he laughed when the question was broached by *The Toronto Sun*. "Well I'm glad to be here. I'm glad to be having a revival and thank you."

In the same *Toronto Sun* piece, Keanu quickly turned philosophical about an attitude that had brought him to this point. "If I read a script and it touches me then I want to do it. If I have an idea and I want to develop it then I'm moved that way."

It was safe to say that roles for Keanu were literally being created with him in mind. Exhibit A? The voice of discarded action figure Duke Caboom in *Toy Story 4*. From the beginning, the filmmakers wanted character of Caboom to be voiced by a Canadian actor, and with that in mind, did blind audio tests with a number of actors reading different lines from the script. Keanu's audition was immediately in the running. He was flown to the Pixar studios for a final meeting and immediately signed on. Keanu was like a little kid in a candy store when he heard the news. "It was a great honor to be invited," he enthused to *The Toronto Sun*. "I was really excited. I knew that by working with and these other characters that I was getting a chance to be a part of something legendary."

While maybe not as legendary as being a part of the Pixar hall of fame, the opportunity to finally go before the cameras for the long anticipated *Bill & Ted Face The Music*, in which the now-middle-aged title characters are visited by a vision from the future that entrusts them with the task of creating a bit of music in 78 minutes that will save the world. Preposterous? Maybe. But definitely in keeping with the spirit, good humor and teen angst of the previous pair of *Bill & Ted* films.

That *Face the Music* took forever to get off the ground was not so much creative differences as the collective peccadillos of the people financing the project. The money people wanted a reboot rather than a direct sequel, and were concerned about the level of international distribution *Face the Music* might receive. Keanu summed it up this way in *Metro:* "Show business is tough. Putting a movie together is tough."

But once the studio moneybags were satisfied, Keanu was all hands on deck and enthusiastic as he offered in interviews with the *NBC Today Show* and *Vanity Fair.* "I think it's pretty surreal playing Bill and Ted at age 50. You can see the life and joy in these characters and I think the world can always use some life and joy. We couldn't be more excited to get the band back together again. There's a lot about Ted that will remain the same. His kind of optimistic naivete in the face of the darkness will still be there. But Ted's had a child now so I'm sure he's matured."

As highly anticipated as a third *Bill & Ted* movie was, it paled next to the announcement in 2019 that *Matrix 4*, once again featuring Keanu as Neo, would soon go into production. *Matrix 4* had been a hot topic in Hollywood since 2015, full of denials, speculation and, at times, a degree of animosity between The Wachowski's and Warner Bros. Through it all, one thing was certain. Despite the fact that Neo allegedly ceased to exist at the end of *Matrix 3: Revolutions*, any

Matrix 4 would have to include Keanu in the role of Neo or risk a potentially angry backlash from Keanu fans.

Keanu knew he was in the catbird seat when he told *TVOM.com* what it would take to get him to do *Matrix 4*. "The Wachowski's would have to be involved. They would have to write it and direct it and then we would have to see where the story was at. Doing another *Matrix* would be weird but why not? People die. Stories don't. People in stories don't."

Early in 2020, it was official and by February the whole *Matrix* universe was excited to hear the news that *Matrix 4*, with extensive scenes involving Keanu would be filming for three weeks in San Francisco. Countless Keanu fans descended on the city. Keanu was seemingly seen everywhere and anywhere. When spotted, it was the image of a bearded, long-haired, very un-Neo-like presence that had the internet agog.

But the production would be conspicuous by how tight-lipped it was being. Little if anything about the story, filming particulars and not much beyond the fact that the core group of original *Matrix* actors had reunited for the occasion, had been leaked to the press. And for his part, Keanu was doing his best to add to the secrecy and the suspense. In fact, when he would say anything about *Matrix 4*, it would be on the high side of vague.

"I'm absolutely excited about *Matrix 4*," he told *Entertainment Weekly*. "It's very ambitious. As it should be."

CHAPTER THIRTY-TWO
KEANU IN 2020? WHO KNOWS

As you are reading this chapter, *Bill & Ted Face the Music* is scheduled to be in theaters on August 20, 2020. But the gods may have other plans and, as such, Keanu's big return to blockbuster status maybe on hold.

The reason? Coronavirus.

The pandemic that came from out of nowhere and is laying waste to the world hit the movie industry particularly hard. Movie and television production ground to a halt and that all-important conduit for getting audiences in the seats, the movie houses, have been shut down since March, by way of an edict to prevent close contact in crowded theaters from spreading the disease.

Consequently, well-thought-out release schedules by the major studios have been thrown out the window. Big tent pole films like the latest James Bond epic, the expected Marvel superhero movies and just about everything Disney had on its schedule have been bumped to much later in 2020 and, in some cases, well into 2021. And even those theaters who are daring to open have been under strict regulation to limit the number of people per showing, often as little as 30 percent of capacity, which would kill a big-budget movie's chances of a big opening weekend.

Long story short. *Bill & Ted Face the Music* may well follow suit but, as of July, the studio is insisting that the film will be released on August 28. So by the time you're reading this, either you've seen *Bill & Ted Face the Music* or you haven't. Simple as that.

But there's more to the Keanu/Coronavirus connection than just *Bill & Ted*. At the time all film production ground to a halt, Keanu was only four weeks into shooting *Matrix 4*, en route to a 2021 release. Following the completion of that film, he was set to jump into filming for the equally anticipated *John Wick 4*, also scheduled for a 2021 release.

In fact, allowing for the eccentricities of Hollywood-think, the Year of Keanu was shaping up for both *Matrix 4* and *John Wick 4* to be released within days of each other. The reality was that it all might be wishful thinking, since *Matrix 4* was nowhere near being completed and *John Wick 4* had not even started. Fortunately saner heads in the John Wick camp upended the logjam that many insiders felt would be an economic disaster. Instead of opening two Keanu films back to back, the studio announced a revamped *John Wick 4* release for 2022.

But that would not be the end of the story. Keanu fanatics continued to fan the flames of all things Keanu, and one group of conspiracy theorists would add to the uncertainty brought on by the Coronavirus, creating one of the more enticing and out-there Keanu stories in quite some time.

Numerous reports from the truncated *Matrix 4* filming, including some photo evidence, showed

Keanu with a very un-Neo like-appearance, complete with a long black coat and very long dark hair. What followed was a literal tidal wave of outrageous but not impossible theories, including speculation that the actor was playing John Wick in some form or fashion in *Matrix 4;* that John Wick has actually been Neo the entire time after inadvertently becoming trapped in a Matrix-style simulation. The most outrageous was the notion that *Matrix 4* and *John Wick 4* would be opening on the same day with a collective storyline that would feature both characters.

The implausibility of all those scenarios, as enticing as they might seem, was not lost on *John Wick* director Chad Stahelski, who gave *Indiewire.com* the low-down on what the actual story was behind the Coronavirus' impact on Keanu's future plans. "*The Matrix* was only four weeks in when all this happened so Keanu's gotta go finish up his commitment on *Matrix 4* which is a big deal and will probably take him until the end of the year. Then we have to go into our prep mode. So release dates. Who knows right now?"

Also hanging in the sky over Keanu during this hiatus was the future of the *John Wick* franchise, which is showing no signs of going away. Keanu was alternately enthusiastic and guarded at how long he wanted to kill everybody in sight. He told *Cinemablend.com* that "The John Wick films are always a lot of fun for me. And as long as they're fun and the stories are interesting, I'll keep doing them." In conversation with *GQ* he acknowledged the dollars and cents of it all. "I'll make more of these films if the demand is there. As far as my legs will take me. As far as the audience wants to go."

Director Stahelski indicated in conversation with *Collider.com* that it was a real question if Keanu would do *John Wick 4*. "Keanu said he was done with the series after *Chapter 3*. We finished the third one and Keanu and I were like 'Okay, it's time to move on. Let's go do a romantic comedy or something. We're good.' Then we got together during a publicity tour in Japan and Keanu goes 'I think I've got one more left in me.' So we were like 'Okay, we'll make a plan.'"

CHAPTER THIRTY-THREE
KEANU: WHO ARE YOU?

Going into 2020, Keanu was an enigma wrapped up in a conundrum, a Rubik's Cube with no answer in sight. Some were convinced that they knew everything about him. Others were equally sure that they knew nothing at all.

And Keanu is no help.

He is literally all over the place at all times. Keanu can be unpredictable, contrary and often subject to spur-of-the-moment thinking that usually makes sense to nobody but Keanu. Keanu is simply Keanu and that's what makes defining what makes him tick so damned difficult. Given the occasion, Keanu has come across as an innocent, a man-child if you will, often cocksure and just as often unsure. To many he's a mental Etch-A-Sketch with ideas, notions and a sense of being that can turn of a dime. And often does.

Looking for insightful and thoughtful Keanu? When television host Stephen Colbert veered away from the typical Hollywood talk show blather to ask Keanu what happens when we die, Keanu turned wise and thoughtful in saying, "I know the ones who love us will miss us." He can also flip a switch and be downright pithy, as chronicled in *Refinery29.com,* when his response to the question of what was his secret for always staying down to earth was "Gravity."

Keanu seemingly has an internal compass primed to take risks. You can see it in his personal life, fast bikes, and often out-of-kilter attitudes and tastes. Over a better than 30- year-career he has regularly alternated full-on smashes with obscurities and oddities that, in a commercial sense, were doomed to fail in every logical way. And when they inevitably did, he would shrug his shoulders and move on to the next.

Get it? If not don't worry. Because when it comes to Keanu you are not alone. Keanu rarely argues with an assessment. He will consider it, file it away or discard it. That's just the way he operates.

Of recent vintage, there's been Keanu the internet dandy whose every seeming waking hour has been chronicled on some website or media outlet. He can be of two minds on it. Sometimes he's appreciative of the attention. But then there are those moments when he gets annoyed at what he perceives as unwarranted attention. "I'm very private," he told *The Guardian*. "So when stuff doesn't stay private, it's not so great."

The many facets of Keanu have continued to defy Hollywood stereotypes at every turn. He's a kind, humble person who works hard at running away from the trappings of celebrity. His A-list celebrity status is undeniable but, in place of ego, material things and arrogance we've come to associate with movie stars, in Keanu we have discovered a real person who is polite, accessible to strangers, to the point, very private, yet very sane, a real person clothed in the celeb life. He made that delineation in conversation with *Zap2It.com* when he said, "I don't want everyone to think of me as a star."

Those who live and die by everything Keanu might well think of him as a very human being. Keanu has seemingly gone through the things we all have. He's loved. He's lost. He's been happy and sad. He's won at certain aspects of life and he's fallen flat on his face in others. If he had not hit the big time in Hollywood, he could have ended up an everyday Joe, somebody who punched a clock, worked a 9 to 5, lived in the suburbs, was behind on his bills and living paycheck to paycheck. He could have been you and me. With Keanu, the possibilities have always been endless.

Through it all, Keanu has remained a universal traveler, wrapped in a sense of both hyper normalcy and a larger-than-life persona, as he moves through an often-unreal and ethereal life. He's at once enticing and maddening, everything and nothing.

It's these traits that have drawn legions of fans and followers across all conceivable lines. His basic coolness and the inexplicability of it all has made him the darling of Millennials, Gen Xers, Generation X, Y and Z kids and, yes, even a smattering of hipsters from the '60s. All have found something in his attitude, more likely an *anti*-attitude, and the way he carries himself, to admire for any number of reasons.

True to his relatable, if somewhat geeky, way of dealing with the world, Keanu was truly in awe when, in a *People* article, he was informed that he had been selected the Internet's Newest Boyfriend. "I've been what? That's wacky. Well the positivity's great."

And it is that adulation that often blurs the line of his true talent. How good an actor Keanu really is has been a line blurred for decades. Even staunch supporters have harbored thoughts of Keanu as a one-trick pony who has essentially played himself in everything he's done. There are just as many who chalk up his on-screen stoicism to real genius. However he does it, one thing is certain: Keanu seems like a natural fit in just about anything he does.

How much any or all of these traits ultimately connect the dots on the character that is Keanu, or simply meld into a surreal mosaic of what people wish or hope he is and will be, remains open to conjecture. Into 2021 and beyond, there maybe a clearer picture... Or maybe the picture will just get a bit fuzzier. But one thing is certain. Keanu will be with us well into the future, a personality of some depth that will continue to evolve and will never be boring

Expect the unexpected. Keanu will always keep the world guessing. Because that's just the way he is.

EPILOGUE
AND PARTY ON!

June 2. 2020.

San Dimas High School was making the best of a difficult situation. The ramifications of the Coronavirus pandemic had taken a toll on the traditions of high school, and the pomp and circumstance of senior year. What was left for those venturing out into an uncertain future was a virtual graduation ceremony played out online.

Shortly before the names of the graduating seniors were to be read, there was a shudder and a crackle on the computer screen. The images of Keanu Reeves and Alex Winter appeared in the virtual verse, all smiles and very Bill and Ted. San Dimas High School had been a touchstone for the storyline in *Bill & Ted* and, in a totally rad and surprising bit of payback, Keanu and Alex decided it would be a nice touch to appear, virtually, at the ceremony and give the graduating class a send off they would never forget.

In a brief message to the student body, Alex acknowledged, "We know that it's a tough time right now and you're having to do this virtual graduation. We want to wish you the best of luck moving forward.

And we wanted to tell you to be excellent to each other."

For his part, Keanu was to the point and very Ted-like when he simply urged, "And party on!"

FILMOGRAPHY

KEANU DID THIS

For completists, the following list features Keanu Reeves' film appearances to date. These include starring and co-starring roles, cameos and voiceover work, for a total of 72 films. The obvious ones as well as a number of obscurities are featured. As this book goes to press, the films listed as 2020 and 2021 releases should be considered tentative. Enjoy.

(2022)

John Wick 4

(2021)

The Matrix IV

(2020)

Bill & Ted Face The Music. The Sponge Bob Movie: Sponge on the Run.

(2019)

Between Two Ferns: The Movie. Toy Story 4. Always Be My Maybe. John Wick: Chapter Three Parabellum.

(2018)
Replicas. Destination Wedding. Siberia.

(2017)
SPF 18. A Happening of Monumental Proportions. John Wick Chapter 2. To The Bone.

(2016)
The Whole Truth. The Bad Batch. The Neon Demon. Exposed.

(2015)
Mifune: The Last Samurai. Deep Web. Knock Knock.

(2014)
John Wick.

(2013)
47 Ronin. Man of Tai Chi.

(2012)
Generation Um… Side by Side…

(2010)
Henry's Crime.

(2009)
The Private Lives of Pippa Lee.

(2008))
The Day The Earth Stood Still. Street Kings.

(2006)

The Great Warming. The Lake House. A Scanner Darkly.

(2005)

Ellie Parker. Thumbsucker. Constantine.

(2003)

Something's Gotta Give. The Matrix: Revolutions. The Matrix: Reloaded.

(2001)

Hardball. Sweet November.

(2000)

The Replacements. The Gift.

(1999)

The Matrix. Me and Will.

(1997)

The Devil's Advocate. The Last Time I Committed Suicide.

(1996)

Feeling Minnesota. Chain Reaction.

(1995)

A Walk in the Clouds. Johnny Mnemonic.

(1994)

Speed.

(1993)

Little Buddha. Freaked. Even Cowgirls Get The Blues. Much Ado About Nothing.

(1992)

Bram Stoker's Dracula.

(1991)

My Own Private Idaho. Bill & Ted's Bogus Journey. Point Break.

(1990)

Tune In Tomorrow. I Love You To Death.

(1989)

Parenthood. Bill & Ted's Excellent Adventure.

(1988)

Dangerous Liaisons. The Prince of Pennsylvania. Permanent Record. The Night Before.

(1986)

River's Edge, Flying. Youngblood.

(1985)

One Step Away.

ROLES KEANU DID NOT GET

Keanu Reeves has been in so many big movies, it's hard to believe that his career is dotted with more than a dozen he either turned down or did not pass muster on with the filmmakers during the audition process. In no particular order, here are the films that Keanu did not get.

PLATOON: Keanu was going through a phase where he did not want to condone or promote violence in his films, which was why he said "thanks but no thanks" when director Oliver Stone came calling with the offer to star in this big-budget Vietnam war film. The role would go to Charlie Sheen.

WATCHMEN: Keanu was cryptic and a bit vague when he acknowledged, "It just didn't work out" as the reason for saying no to the role of Dr. Manhattan, which ultimately went to Billy Crudup.

WOLVERINE: Keanu really wanted this role and seemed to have a shot when the original actor Dougray Scott dropped out of the project. But Hugh Jackman stepped in at the last possible moment and snatched the prize away.

FAIR GAME: Keanu displayed either good sense or second sight when he turned down the opportunity to play opposite Cindy Crawford in this romantic thriller. Long story short, *Fair Game* was a bomb of massive proportions and Keanu's career was still intact.

SPEED RACER: Even the opportunity to once again work with *Matrix* directors the Wachowski brothers was not enough to get Keanu to say yes to the role of Racer X in *Speed Racer*.

BOWFINGER: Keanu fell victim to Hollywood power and politics when the role of Kit Reeves was essentially handed to him on a silver platter by the film's star and writer Steve Martin. But when producer Brian Grazer read the script, he handed the role to Eddie Murphy.

THE ETERNALS: Keanu thought it would be a hoot to be in a film with Angelina Jolie. But he had just too much on his plate and could not fit the film in. Poor Keanu.

THE FLY II: The company wanted Keanu for this sequel. Keanu hated the script. End of story.

TROPIC THUNDER: The role of Tugg Speedman was Keanu's right up to the moment when director Ben Stiller decided he wanted the role.

CAPTAIN MARVEL: The opportunity to play Yon Rogg, Captain Marvel's mentor, was there for the taking. Only one thing got in the way, a trifle named *John Wick 3*.

SPIDER MAN: FAR FROM HOME: It's become an almost annual event. Marvel casts another film and they immediately knock on Keanu's door. This time was no different than the previous dances. Marvel made the offer. Keanu turned it down.

THE OBJECT OF MY AFFECTION: Sometimes Keanu just simply changed his mind. The lead in this film was one of those times. Even with the temptation of playing opposite Uma Thurman, Keanu finally decided against it.

SPEED 2: CRUISE CONTROL: It's rare that anybody pisses off more people in the movie biz than Keanu did with this film. He hated the script and he saw making this dog as a career-ender. He turned down big bucks in favor of integrity.

THE LORD OF THE RINGS: THE FELLOWSHIP OF THE RINGS: Keanu wanted the role of Aragon so bad he could taste it. Sadly, the decision makers decided that Viggo Mortensen was a better choice.

HEAT: Keanu turned down a large payday and major role in this film in favor of a short run in a Canadian theater production of *Hamlet* for peanuts. Keanu preferred the Bard, so it made perfect sense.

CHICAGO: Director Rob Marshall wanted Keanu for the role of Amos Hart. John C. Reilly got the part.

CUTTHROAT ISLAND: Keanu auditioned for the role of William in this swashbuckler, but ultimately lost out to Matthew Modine.

ENCHANTED: Keanu had the part in his hot little hands but turned it down. Who out there remembers *Enchanted*?

SHOOTER: Keanu was caught in the middle on this one. He had the part at a time when the production was in limbo. By the time production resumed, Keanu had moved on to other things.

STOMPANATO: A really obscure bit of business in which Keanu was set to star as the lowlife lover of Lana Turner. The movie was never made.

SOURCES
INTERVIEWS

Many thanks to Professor William Irwin for his insightful and enlightening interview.

BOOKS
The New Breed of Actors Coming of Age by Karen Hardy Bystedt and Kevin J. Koffler. *Keanu* by Sheila Johnston. *It's Messy: Essays on Boys, Boobs and Badass Women* by Amanda De Cadenet.

MAGAZINES
Vogue UK, Vanity Fair, TV Week, US, Penthouse, Rolling Stone, Total Film, People, Dolly, Esquire, TV Park, Choices, The Express On Sunday, MacLeans, Interview, Girlfriend, BB, Empire, Vice, Film Review, Choices, Parade, W, Star, Entertainment Weekly, Newsday, Another Man, Starlog, Movieline, ETC, Paper, Tele 7 Jours, The Star, Just 17, Detour, Time Out London, Hello, Ladies Home Journal, New Weekly, Now, Wired, Martialarm Martial Arts, Blue, Grazia, Cosmopolitan, Woman's Day, Stern, Vogue Spain, Esquire UK, Big Life, Playgirl, GQ.

NEWSPAPERS/WIRE SERVICES

Page Six. Honolulu Star Bulletin, Toronto Sun, The Daily Beast, The Globe And Mail, The Daily Mail, Los Angeles Times, USA Today, Gannett News Service, Boston Globe, Jakarta Post, The Telegraph, Winnipeg Free Press, Wall Street Journal, New York Post, The Morning Call, Calgary Sun, London Evening Standard, Chicago Sun Times, WENN Syndicate, The Times, National Enquirer, United Press International, Reuters, Associated Press, The Daily Beast, New York Times, The Korea Times, The Korea Herald, Women's Health, Belfast Telegraph, Metro.

WEBSITES

Goalcast.com, BrainyQuote.com, PickABrain.com, RedditOnline.com, Collider.com, Cinemablend.com, HerMoments.com, DyslexiaHelp.com, Handbag.com, Whoaisnotme.com, Looper.com, YoungAmericans.com, Obnoxious&Anonymous.com, Lizismile.com, T&B.com, TheMind'sJournal.com, SFGate.com, BlackBook.com, Paloaltoonline.com, MyRiverPhoenixCollection.com, Movielab.com, Star2.com,Hollywood.com, Zap2It.com, UPROXX.com, MSN.com, Brampton Guardian.com, Beliefnet.com, Vulture.com, TVOM.com, Female.com, Contactmusic.com, The Wrap.com, ArizonaCentral.com, Cover Media.com, Mr.Reeves.com, Popsugar.com, Cheatsheet.com, Comingsoon.net, Screenrant.com, KeanuIsImmortal.com, Tentstile.com, Refinery29.com. BBC News.com, IndeLondon.com, ENews.com,

TELEVISION

The Late Show with James Corden, The Tonight Show With Jimmy Fallon, Entertainment Tonight, The Today Show, Ellen DeGeneres Show, ABC News, GMA Network.

About the Author

New York Times bestselling author Marc Shapiro has written more than 60 nonfiction celebrity biographies, more than 24 comic books, numerous short stories and poetry, and three short-form screenplays. He is also a veteran freelance entertainment journalist.

His young adult book, *JK Rowling: The Wizard Behind Harry Potter,* was on *The New York Times* bestseller list for four straight weeks. His fact-based book *Total Titanic* was also on *The Los Angeles Times* bestseller list for four weeks. *Justin Bieber: The Fever* was on the nationwide Canadian bestseller list for several weeks.

Shapiro has written books on such personalities as Shonda Rhimes, George Harrison, Carlos Santana, Annette Funicello, Lorde, Lindsay Johan, E.L. James, Jamie Dornan, Dakota Johnson, Adele and countless others. He also co-authored the autobiography of mixed martial arts fighter Tito Ortiz, *This Is Gonna Hurt: The Life of a Mixed Martial Arts Champion.*

He is currently working on group biographies of Beatle Wives and Beatle Kids for Riverdale Avenue Books.

Other Riverdale Avenue Books Titles
by Marc Shapiro

Hard Work: The Greta Van Fleet Story

Lorde: Your Heroine, How This Young Feminist Broke the Rules and Succeeded

Legally Bieber: Justin Bieber at 18

You're Gonna Make It After All: The Life, Times and Influence of Mary Tyler Moore

Hey Joe: The Unauthorized Biography of a Rock Classic

Trump This! The Life and Times of Donald Trump, an Unauthorized Biography

The Secret Life of EL James

The Real Steele: The Unauthorized Biography of Dakota Johnson

Inside Grey's Anatomy: The Unauthorized Biography of Jamie Dornan

Annette Funicello: America's Sweetheart

Game: The Resurrection of Tim Tebow

*Lindsay Lohan: Fully Loaded,
From Disney to Disaster*

Jenni: An Unauthorized Biography

Who Is Katie Holmes? An Unauthorized Biography

*Norman Reedus: True Tales of
The Waking Dead's Zombie Hunter,
An Unauthorized Biography*

*Welcome to Shondaland: An Unauthorized
Biography of Shonda Rhimes*

Renaissance Man: The Lin Manuel Story

John McCain: View from the Hill

Printed in Great Britain
by Amazon